knitted
socks

Anna Tillman

knitted
socks

Over 25 designs
for fab feet and
cozy toes for the
whole family

TRAFALGAR SQUARE
North Pomfret, Vermont

First published in the United States of America in 2008 by
Trafalgar Square Books, North Pomfret, Vermont 05053

Printed in China

Copyright © Octopus Publishing Group Ltd 2008

Library of Congress Control Number: 2007906372

ISBN-13: 978-1-57076-386-1

10 9 8 7 6 5 4 3 2 1

contents

introduction

Despite growing up in a family of knitters, no one ever showed me how to knit socks. I was aware from a young age that it was possible to knit them but, because they can't be broken down into flat pieces, I was never encouraged to try them. Finally, I worked up the nerve to try a pair, and was delighted when I turned my first heel! It may look like some mystical powers are required to knit a three-dimensional shape that fits your foot, but it's just not true. The basics of knit and purl, increasing and decreasing are all you need for a perfect fit.

This book aims to give you all the information you need to start creating beautiful socks. Most of the patterns in the book have a large range of sizes, and Getting the Right Size table (opposite), will help you pick the correct one. The Sock-Knitting Basics section (see pages 8–15) not only includes advice on sock knitting, but also fully explains the different parts of socks.

There are projects here to suit all abilities and tastes. If you are a novice sock knitter, try something simple yet effective, like the dazzling Crazy Fur socks on page 28. The elegant Slouch Socks on page 84 take little more knitting skill, while for more of a challenge the Going Dotty pair on page 74 is reversible. Few little girls can resist the Sock Buddies on page 50, and there are textures and designs, including lace and Fair Isle, to work.

If knitting some of the projects makes you itch to design your own socks, then turn to pages 134–141. Here you will find pattern instructions for the different ways the basic elements of socks – such as cuffs, heels and toes – can be knitted, and you can combine these interchangeable parts to create your very own unique pair of socks.

Not only are socks the ultimate in 'impress your friends' knitting, they have many other advantages. A sock project often consists of one ball of yarn and some needles, so it is perfect for tucking in a bag and knitting on the go. Socks are not a huge expense to knit, nor will they take months to complete. Possibly best of all, most of us wear socks so a pair of hand-knitted socks is a unique and personal gift that you know will be appreciated.

getting the right size

There is no one standard conversion table for all international shoe sizes: the more different charts you look at, the more variations you will get, though usually only to within one size. Fortunately, socks are by their very nature stretchy, so the precise fit needed for shoes is not essential for socks.

These tables will help you choose a size to knit your project to.

Children's sizes	CS	CM	CL	CXL
USA sizes	4½–6½	7½–9½	10½–12½	13½–3½
UK sizes	4–6	7–9	10–12	13–3
Aus sizes	3½–5½	6½–8½	9½–11½	12½–2½
European sizes	20–23	24–26	27–31	32–35

Adult sizes	AS	AM	AL	AXL
US (men's sizes), Aus and UK (men's and ladies sizes)	4–6	7–9	10–12	13–14
USA women's sizes	5½–7½	8½–10½	11½–13½	14½–15½
Aus women's sizes	6–8	9–11	12–14	14–16
European sizes	35–39	40–43	44–46	47–48

sock-knitting basics

Novice knitters are often put off knitting socks because they seem too complicated, and you have to deal with all those needles! However, socks can be thought of in simple sections – Rib, Cuff, Heel, Foot and Toe – and you are actually only knitting on two needles at a time, the others can just be ignored until you need them. Here is a guide to the structure of a knitted sock and how to knit it.

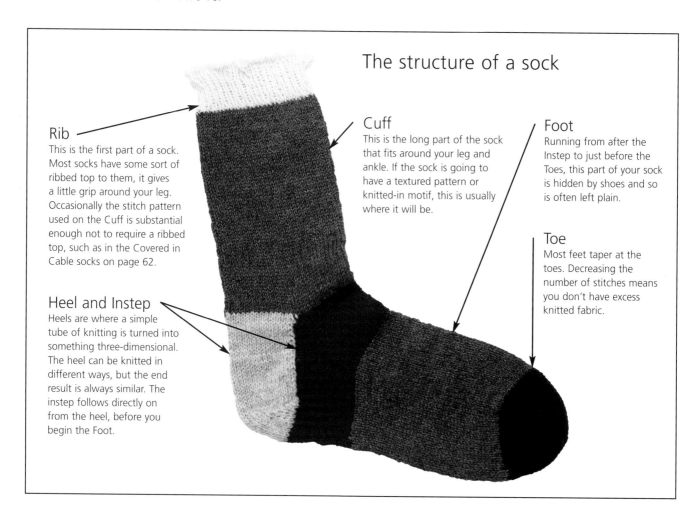

The structure of a sock

Rib
This is the first part of a sock. Most socks have some sort of ribbed top to them, it gives a little grip around your leg. Occasionally the stitch pattern used on the Cuff is substantial enough not to require a ribbed top, such as in the Covered in Cable socks on page 62.

Cuff
This is the long part of the sock that fits around your leg and ankle. If the sock is going to have a textured pattern or knitted-in motif, this is usually where it will be.

Foot
Running from after the Instep to just before the Toes, this part of your sock is hidden by shoes and so is often left plain.

Toe
Most feet taper at the toes. Decreasing the number of stitches means you don't have excess knitted fabric.

Heel and Instep
Heels are where a simple tube of knitting is turned into something three-dimensional. The heel can be knitted in different ways, but the end result is always similar. The instep follows directly on from the heel, before you begin the Foot.

Getting started

There is little difference between knitting a sock and knitting any other project, but here are some techniques that you will find useful.

Casting on

The cast-on edge of a sock needs to be fairly elastic as it has to slide easily over your heel and ankle yet sit snugly around your leg as well. Most of the well-known methods of casting on are fine for socks, although each has its own strengths. The cable cast on method, gives you a neat, firm edge that looks good, but can be a little tight for the top of socks, so if you tend to cast on tightly, use needles one size larger than those you will use for the rest of the socks. There are also two simple, stretchy cast-on methods described on page 136 which can be used with most sock patterns.

Knitting in the round

The majority of socks in this book are knitted in the round. This creates a smooth, seam-free sock that is comfortable to wear. The patterns suggest four double-pointed needles, but some people prefer five and occasionally it is easier to add an additional spare to help hold stitches – it is up to you to decide what suits you best.

There are also various methods of knitting socks on circular needles (magic loop, two circulars or short circular needles), and all the patterns in this book can be knitted on circular needles if you prefer.

Whichever method you choose, it is much easier to cast on all the stitches on one needle, then divide them between needles, making sure you don't twist the row of cast-on stitches.

One easy way of getting started knitting in the round is to cast on one more stitch than you require. Once you have divided up the stitches on the needles, slip the last stitch onto the same needle as the first one, then knit these two stitches together.

Using markers

When you are knitting in the round it helps to have a method of keeping track of the beginning of the rounds. The patterns in this book use markers placed at the beginning of the round and at key points in the shaping. There are different styles of marker available, but when knitting socks you want something that is going to travel up the work with you to mark the specified positions in the round you are working on. Ring markers that slide onto the needles between stitches are great for this and are readily available, but a loop of scrap yarn can be just as effective.

Kitchener stitch (also known as grafting)

Grafting stitches together at the toe of socks gives a seamless finish. Kitchener stitch mimics an additional row of knitting between the stitches and, although the instructions can seem daunting at first, they follow a logical sequence pattern that is not difficult to master.

Cut yarn leaving a long tail and thread through a tapestry needle.

Hold the two knitting needles with stitches on together, parallel to one another, with the one the tail comes from at the back. The tail must always be on the right-hand side of the knitting.

Insert tapestry needle purlwise into first stitch on the front needle.
Pull yarn through, leaving stitch on needle.
Insert tapestry needle knitwise into first stitch on the back needle.
Pull yarn through, leaving stitch on needle.
*Insert tapestry needle knitwise into first stitch on the front needle and slip stitch off needle.
Insert tapestry needle purlwise into next stitch on the front needle.
Pull yarn through, leaving stitch on needle.
Insert tapestry needle purlwise into first stitch on the back needle and slip stitch off needle.
Insert tapestry needle knitwise into next stitch on the back needle.
Pull yarn through, leaving stitch on needle.
Rep from * until all stitches have been grafted.

Sometimes you will find that when you hold the needles together the yarn tail will come from the stitch on the front needle. In which case graft the stitches as follows:

Insert tapestry needle knitwise into first stitch on the back needle. Pull yarn through, leaving stitch on needle.
Insert tapestry needle purlwise into first stitch on the front needle. Pull yarn through, leaving stitch on needle.
*Insert tapestry needle purlwise into first stitch on the back needle and slip stitch off needle.
Insert tapestry needle knitwise into next stitch on the back needle. Pull yarn through, leaving stitch on needle.
Insert tapestry needle knitwise into first stitch on the front needle and slip stitch off needle.
Insert tapestry needle purlwise into next stitch on the front needle. Pull yarn through, leaving stitch on needle.
Rep from * until all sts have been grafted.

Finishing techniques

When you have spent many hours knitting, it is essential that you complete your project correctly for the best final result. Follow the simple instructions provided here to achieve a beautifully finished sock.

Pressing

It is not always necessary to press your socks. If they are knitted in the round and the toes are Kitchener stitched, you can put them right on. However, pressing will make those that require sewing up easier to complete.

With the wrong side of the fabric face-up, pin out each knitted piece on an ironing board, easing it to fit the measurements given. If specific measurements are not provided for your project, pin out your knitting neatly without overstretching it and unfurl any edges that may be rolling up.

Because each yarn is different, refer to the ball band and press your knitted pieces according to the manufacturer's instructions – take special care if your yarn contains acrylic, as it may not be suitable for pressing. Always use a cloth between the knitting and iron to avoid scorching. Lightly press or steam the knitted fabric. If you steam your knitting, remember to let it dry completely before removing the pins.

Sewing in ends

Once you have pressed your finished pieces, you will need to sew in all the loose ends of yarn. Sew in all ends and don't be tempted to use a long yarn end for sewing up. Always use a separate length of yarn for this task so that if you make a mistake, you can undo the stitching without the danger of unravelling all your knitting.

Thread a tapestry needle with the loose end of the yarn, weave the needle through about five stitches on the wrong side of the fabric and pull the yarn through. Weave the needle in the opposite direction for about five stitches, pull the yarn through again and cut off the end neatly with scissors.

Sewing up

There are several ways of joining pieces of knitting, the most common ways are flat seaming with mattress stitch and backstitch, which makes a raised seam. Flat seaming is used for ribs, but otherwise the two are interchangeable.

Mattress stitch

Mattress stitch is a method of joining knitted pieces from the right side of the fabric and is ideal for matching stripes accurately. For the best finish, this stitch should be worked one stitch in from the edge of the knitting.

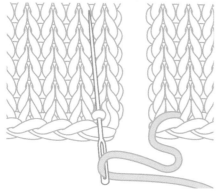  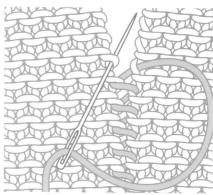

1 With the right sides of the knitting face-up, lay the pieces to be joined edge to edge. From the wrong side on the first row, insert a tapestry needle between the edge stitch and the second stitch. Take the yarn to the opposite piece, insert the needle from the front between the edge stitch and the second stitch of the first row, pass the needle under the loops of two rows and bring it back through to the front.

2 Insert the needle under the loops of the corresponding two rows in the opposite piece in the same way as in step 1. Continue this zigzag lacing all along the seam, taking care not to miss any rows and matching any pattern carefully.

3 Pull the yarn to close the seam, either after each action or after a few stitches. Take care not to pull it too tight, or the seam will pucker, or leave it too loose.

Backstitch

Backstitch is the other main method of making up a piece of knitting. It is worked from the wrong side of the knitted fabric.

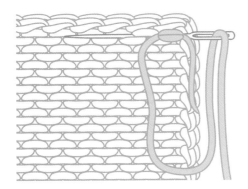

1 Pin the pieces to be joined with right-sides facing. Insert a tapestry needle between the first two stitches at one end, one stitch or row from the edge. Take the needle around the two edges and insert it at the same place as before to secure the yarn end. Insert the needle just behind where it last came out, make a small stitch across the back of the work, bringing the needle through to the front again at the end of the stitch.

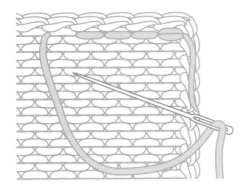

2 Re-insert the needle where the previous stitch ended. Take it across the back of the work for the width of two stitches, then bring it through to the front. Repeat this step to the end of the seam, taking care to match any pattern.

Choosing yarns

It is now possible to purchase yarns in two different ways: from yarn shops and via the Internet (search for 'knitting yarns'). Both sources offer a huge range of yarns and other products, such as needles, buttons, beads and other accessories.

If you are a knitting novice it is a good idea to visit a yarn shop, where you will be amazed at the vast array of yarns available. You will be able to touch the different balls of yarn and examine their textures, become familiar with all the different types on offer and discuss your requirements with the knowledgeable staff. A good Internet site is a fantastic resource, too: it will display the whole spectrum of colors in a yarn range and provide plenty of useful knitting information. You will also often be able to order shade cards, which will help you get a feel for the yarns available.

The problem comes in deciding which yarns to choose from the multitude on offer. In the knitting patterns in this book I have specified the yarn I have used, as it is often the particular texture and/or colors that inspired the design. I have used a variety of different sock yarns: some for practical reasons, some because of the color range, and some because they are just so luxurious.

There is a huge range of yarns that are designed specifically for sock knitting. Many contain a proportion of man-made fiber for durability and ease of washing. Others may be treated or spun in a particular way to make them hardwearing. Choose your yarn carefully as, although it is possible to create socks in any yarn of a suitable weight, you will want to consider how easy they will be care for and how long they will last.

Substituting yarns

You may wish to substitute the yarn I have used in a pattern with one of your own choice. You will need to take care if you do this, because all the patterns are worked out mathematically to the specified yarn.

Yarns come in various weights, such as 4-ply, double knitting and Aran. If you are substituting one yarn for another, look for a similar yarn with the same gauge/tension – this will be stated on the ball band. Always knit a gauge/tension square of your chosen yarn before embarking on the design as if you do not achieve the gauge/tension stated in the pattern, your project will knit up too big or too small.

Some yarns are not easy to substitute. For example, I would not recommend the substitution of another yarn for Felted Slipper Socks (see pages 96–99), as other yarns may not felt to the same degree as the yarn suggested in this pattern.

Having said all this, it can be fun to substitute yarns and to start thinking creatively about knitting.

Working from a chart

Some of the designs in this book include both written instructions and a chart. To write out the whole pattern would be very complicated, and it is usually just as easy to visualize your knitting as a chart and begin to treat it as a picture, 'painting' with the different-colored yarns.

Reading a chart is easier if you imagine it as the right side of a piece of knitting, working from the lower edge to the top. Each square on the chart represents one stitch, and each line of squares represents one row of knitting. Each yarn color used is given a letter in the pattern, which corresponds with a symbol on the chart. This is shown in the key that accompanies the chart.

When knitting a flat piece of fabric from a chart, as for Pop-out Penguins (see pages 18–23) and The Whole Hog (see pages 32–37), read odd-numbered rows – 1, 3, 5 etc (the right side of the fabric) – from right to left, and even-numbered rows – 2, 4, 6 etc (the wrong side of the fabric) – from left to right.

When working from a chart in the round, the right side of the fabric will always be facing you and you should read ALL chart rows from right to left.

When knitting flat

When knitting in the round

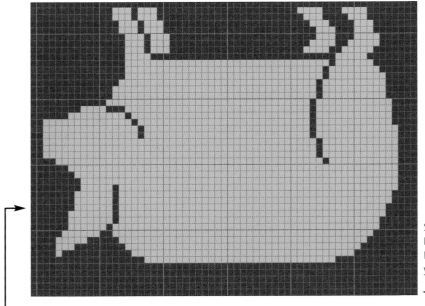

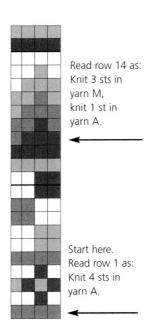

Read row 14 as:
Knit 3 sts in yarn M, knit 1 st in yarn A.

Start here.
Read row 1 as:
Knit 4 sts in yarn A.

Start here.
Read row 1 as:
Knit 61 sts in yarn A.

Read row 14 as:

Purl 7 sts in yarn A, purl 6 sts in yarn B, purl 1 st in yarn A, purl 42 sts in yarn B, purl 5 sts in yarn A.

fabulous
feet

pop-out **penguins**

These little fellas have three-dimensional beaks, flippers and tails and make a really fun pair of socks. Wear them with sandals to show off your perky penguins.

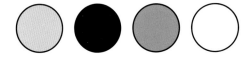

Sizes
CXL (AS:AM:AL:AXL)
(See page 7.)

Materials
2 (2:2:2:2) 1¾oz (50 g) balls of Schoeller & Stahl Fortissima in main color M (pale blue/Ice 1004) and 1 (1:1:1:1) ball each in A (black/Black 1002), B (yellow/Maize 1007) and C (white/Brilliant White 1024)
Pair of US 2 (2.75 mm) knitting needles
Set of US 2 (2.75 mm) double-pointed knitting needles

Gauge/Tension
36 sts and 44 rows to 4 in (10 cm) over stockinette/stocking stitch using US 2 (2.75 mm) needles

Abbreviations
cm centimeter(s); **cont** continu(e)(ing); **g** gram(s); **in** inch(es); **k** knit; **mm** millimeter; **oz** ounce(s); **p** purl; **rep** repeat; **RS** right side; **sl1** slip one stitch; **ssk2tog** [slip next stitch] twice, insert left needle into front of slipped stitches and knit together; **st(s)** stitch(es); **tog** together; **wrap next st** wrap next stitch by slipping next stitch from left to right needle, take yarn to opposite side of work between needles, slip stitch back onto the left needle – when working wrapped stitches, work through both the stitch and the wrap.

Socks (both alike)
Using US 2 (2.75 mm) knitting needles and yarn M, cast on 57 (61:65:69:73) sts.

Rib
Row 1 (RS) K1, [p1, k1] to end.
Row 2 P1, [k1, p1] to end.
Rep these last two rows 7 more times.

Cuff
Place Charts
Chart row 1 Using yarn M k1 (3:5:7:9), k Chart A row 1, using yarn M k1 (3:5:7:9), k Chart B row 1.
Chart row 2 P Chart B row 2, using yarn M p1 (3:5:7:9), p Chart A row 2, using yarn M p1 (3:5:7:9).
These rows place Charts. Cont as set until Charts A and B row 9 is complete.
Chart row 10 P Chart B row 10, using yarn A, p1 (3:5:7:9), p Chart A row 10, using yarn A, p1 (3:5:7:9).
Cont as set until Charts are complete, working the green, red and purple Chart stitches as follows:

Green – Beak
Do not break yarn A.
Using yarn B, purl across the 8 sts shown in green, turn.
Row 1 K7, wrap next st, turn.
Row 2 P6, wrap next st, turn.
Row 3 K5, wrap next st, turn.
Row 4 P4, wrap next st, turn.
Row 5 K3, wrap next st, turn.
Row 6 P2, wrap next st, turn.
Row 7 K2, work wrapped st, turn.
Row 8 P3, work wrapped st, turn.
Row 9 K4, work wrapped st, turn.
Row 10 P5, work wrapped st, turn.
Row 11 K6, work wrapped st, turn.
Row 12 P7, work wrapped st, turn.
Row 13 K8, turn.
Break off yarn B, pick up yarn A and purl across 8 beak

sts and to end of Chart row 12.

Red – Flippers
Using yarn A, purl across the 8 sts shown in red, turn.
Row 1 K7, wrap next st, turn.
Row 2 P6, wrap next st, turn.
Row 3 K6, wrap next st, turn.
Row 4 P6, wrap next st, turn.
Row 5 K5, wrap next st, turn.
Row 6 P4, wrap next st, turn.
Row 7 K4, wrap next st, turn.
Row 8 P4, wrap next st, turn.
Row 9 K3, wrap next st, turn.
Row 10 P2, wrap next st, turn.
Row 11 K2, work wrapped st, turn.
Row 12 P3, work wrapped st, turn.
Row 13 K4, work wrapped st, turn.
Row 14 P5, work wrapped st, turn.
Row 15 K6, turn.
Row 16 P6, turn.
Row 17 K6, work wrapped st, turn.
Row 18 P7, work wrapped st.
Complete chart row 34 making 2nd flipper in same way.

Purple – Tail
Using yarn A, purl acoss the 12 sts shown in purple, turn.
Row 1 K10, wrap next st, turn.
Row 2 P8, wrap next st, turn.
Row 3 K6, wrap next st, turn.
Row 4 P4, wrap next st, turn.
Row 5 K3, wrap next st, turn.
Row 6 P2, wrap next st, turn.
Row 7 K2, work wrapped st, turn.
Row 8 P3, work wrapped st, turn.
Row 9 K4, work wrapped st, turn.
Row 10 P6, work wrapped st, turn.
Row 11 K8, work wrapped st, turn.

Pop-out penguins sock charts

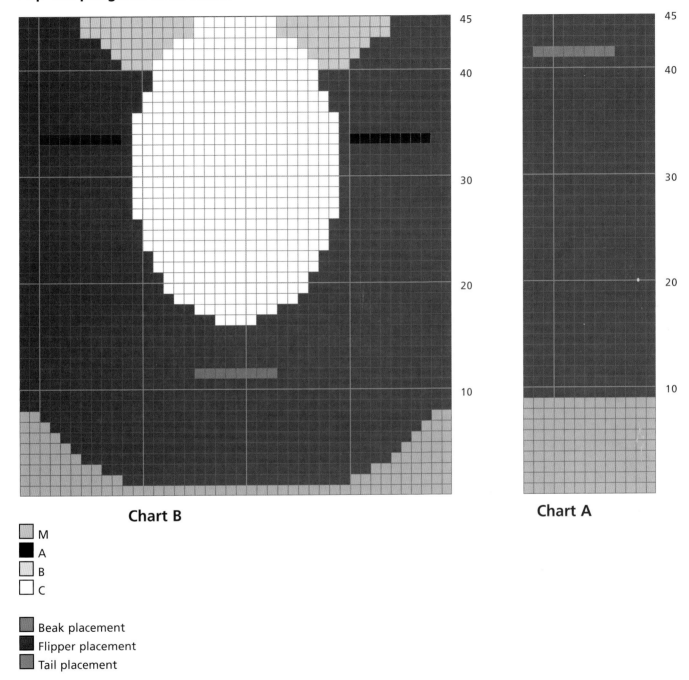

Chart B

Chart A

☐ M
■ A
☐ B
☐ C

▨ Beak placement
▨ Flipper placement
▨ Tail placement

Row 12 P10, work wrapped st, turn.
Row 13 K, turn.
Using yarn A, purl to end of Chart row 42.

Once Chart is complete break off all contrast yarns and using yarn M, purl 1 row.

Joining row K56 (60:64:68:72), slip sts onto US 2 (2.75 mm) double-pointed needles.
Divide sts between 3 needles and knit last st and first st together to join work into the round. 56 (60:64:68:72) sts.
Knit to and place marker at point shown by orange line on Chart A (this will mark the beginning of each round).

Heel flap
K14 (15:16:17:18), turn.
Row 1 Sl1, p27 (29:31:33:35), turn.
Slide other 28 (30:32:34:36) sts onto spare needles.
Row 2 Sl1, k27 (29:31:33:35).
Working in rows on these 28 (30:32:34:36) sts, rep these last 2 rows 13 (14:15:16:17) more times.

Heel shaping
Row 1 Sl1, p15 (16:17:18:19), p2tog, p1, turn.
Row 2 Sl1, k5, ssk2tog, k1, turn.
Row 3 Sl1, p6, p2tog, p1, turn.
Row 4 Sl1, k7, ssk2tog, k1, turn.
Cont in this way, taking one more stitch in each row until the row 'Sl1, k13 (15:15:17:17), ssktog, k1, turn' has been worked. (For AS and AL, do NOT turn at end of this last row.)
CXL, AM, AXL only:
Next row Sl1, p14(-:16:-:18), p2tog, turn.
Next row Sl1, k14(-:16:-:18), ssk2tog.
All Sizes: 16 (18:18:20:20) sts.

Pick up for instep
Pick up knitwise 14 (15:16:17:18) sts down side of heel flap, place marker,
Knit across 28 (30:32:34:36) sts from cuff, place marker, pick up knitwise 14 (15:16:17:18) sts up side of heel flap, knit to end of round. 72 (78:82:88:92) sts.

Shape instep
Round 1 Knit to 3 sts before first marker, k2tog, k1 (marker), knit to next marker, k1, ssk2tog, knit to end.
Round 2 Knit.
Rep these last two rounds until 56 (60:64:68:72) sts remain.

Foot
Knit 42 (45:48:51:54) rounds.

Decrease for toe
Round 1 Knit to 3 sts before first marker, k2tog, k1 (marker), k1, ssk2tog, knit to 3 sts before next marker, k2tog, k1 (marker), k1, ssk2tog, knit to end. 52 (56:60:64:68) sts.
Round 2 Knit.
Rep these last two rounds until 24 sts remain.
Knit to first marker.

Rearrange sts so that the first 6 and last 6 sts of the round are on one needle with the 12 middle sts on another needle.
Graft toe together using Kitchener stitch (see page 10).

Finishing
Sew in all ends.
Join cuff seam.
Using photograph as a guide, embroider eyes using yarn C.

strawberries **& cream**

Delicate strawberries and leaf motifs transform an easy-to-knit cream sock into a wonderfully eye-catching design – you could even just make the motifs and sew them onto a ready-made pair of socks.

Sizes

CS (CM:CL:CXL:AS:AM:AL)

(See page 7.)

Materials

2 (2:2:2:3:3:4) 1¾ oz (50 g) balls of Regia Silk 6-ply in cream/Natural 002 and oddments in green, red and yellow for decoration

Set of US 3 (3.25 mm) double-pointed knitting needles

Set of US 2½ (3 mm) double-pointed knitting needles

Pair of US 2½ (3 mm) knitting needles

Small amount toy filling

Gauge/Tension

24 sts and 34 rows to 4 in (10 cm) over stockinette/stocking stitch using US 3 (3.25 mm) needles

Abbreviations

cm centimeter(s); **g** gram(s); **in** inch(es); **inc** increase; **k** knit; **M1** make one by inserting left needle under strand between needles and working into the back of it; **mm** millimeter; **oz** ounce(s); **p** purl; **p2sso** pass two slipped stitches over; **rep** repeat; **RS** right side; **sl1** slip one stitch; **sl2** slip two stitches; **ssk2tog** [slip next stitch] twice, insert left needle into front of slipped stitches and knit together; **st(s)** stitch(es); **tog** together.

Socks (both alike)

Using US 3 (3.25 mm) double-pointed needles, cast on 32 (36:40:44:48:52:56) sts.
Divide sts between 3 needles, join and place marker.

Rib

Working in the round:
Round 1 (RS) *K1, p1, rep from * to end.
Rep this last round 14 more times.

Cuff

Knit 36 (40:44:48:56:64:68) rounds.

Heel flap

K8 (9:10:11:12:13:14), turn.
Row 1 Sl1, p15 (17:19:21:23:25:27), turn.
Slide other 16 (18:20:22:24:26:28) sts onto spare needles.
Row 2 Sl1, k15 (17:19:21:23:25:27), turn.
Working back and forth on these 16 (18:20:22:24:26:28) sts, rep these last two rows 7 (8:9:10:11:12:13) more times.

Heel shaping

Row 1 Sl1, p9 (10:11:12:13:14:15), p2tog, p1, turn.
Row 2 Sl1, k5, ssk2tog, k1, turn.
Row 3 Sl1, p6, p2tog, p1, turn.
Row 4 Sl1, k7, ssk2tog, k1, turn.
Rep last 2 rows 0 (1:1:2:2:3:3) times more. (For CM, CXL and AM, do NOT turn at end of last row.)
CS, CL, AS, AL only:
Next row Sl1, p8(-:10:-:12:-:14), p2tog, turn.
Next row Sl1, k8(-:10:-:12:-:14), ssk2tog.
All Sizes: 10 (12:12:14:14:16:16) sts.

Pick up for instep

Pick up knitwise 8 (9:10:11:12:13:14) sts down side of heel flap, place marker.
Knit 16 (18:20:22:24:26:28) sts from cuff, place marker, pick up knitwise 8 (9:10:11:12:13:14) sts up side of heel flap,
Knit to end of round. 42 (48:52:58:62:68:72) sts.

Shape instep

Round 1 Knit to 3 sts before first marker, k2tog, k1 (marker), knit to next marker (marker), k1, ssk2tog, knit to end. 40 (46:50:56:60:66:70) sts.
Round 2 Knit.
Rep these last two rounds until 32 (36:40:44:48:52:56) sts remain.

Foot

Knit 20 (24:28:32:40:48:56) rounds.

Decrease for toe

Round 1 Knit to 3 sts before first marker, k2tog, k1 (marker), k1, ssk2tog, knit to 3 sts before next marker, k2tog, k1 (marker), k1, ssk2tog, knit to end. 28 (32:36:40:44:48:52) sts.
Round 2 Knit.
Rep these last two rounds until 16 sts remain.
Knit to first marker.
Rearrange sts so that the first 4 and last 4 sts of the round are on one needle with the 8 middle sts on another needle.
Graft toe together using Kitchener stitch (see page 10).
Sew in all ends.

Strawberries

(make 4)

Using US 2½ (3 mm) double-pointed needles and red yarn, cast on 8 sts.

Divide sts between 3 needles, join and place marker. Working in the round:

Round 1 Inc once in each st to end. 16 sts.

Knit 6 rounds.

Round 8 [K2tog] to end. 8 sts.

Break yarn, thread through remaining sts, draw up tightly and secure end.

Stuff lightly with toy filling and close cast-on edge.

Using green yarn, embroider lazy daisy stitches to form calyx.

Using yellow yarn, embroider short, straight-stitch seeds at random over the strawberry.

Leaf sprays

(make 2)

Using US 2½ (3 mm) needles and green yarn, cast on 4 sts.

Row 1 K1, inc once in each of last 3 sts. 7 sts.

Row 2 and all following even rows Purl.

Row 3 K2, M1, k3, M1, k2. 9 sts.

Row 5 K3, sl2, k1, p2sso, k3. 7 sts.

Row 7 K2, sl2, k1, p2sso, k2. 5 sts.

Row 8 Purl, leaving sts on the needle.

Make two more leaves. After row 8 of third leaf, break yarn, thread through sts of all leaves, draw up tightly and secure.

Finishing

Using photograph as a guide, sew two strawberries and a leaf spray to the ankle of each sock. Using green yarn, embroider stems.

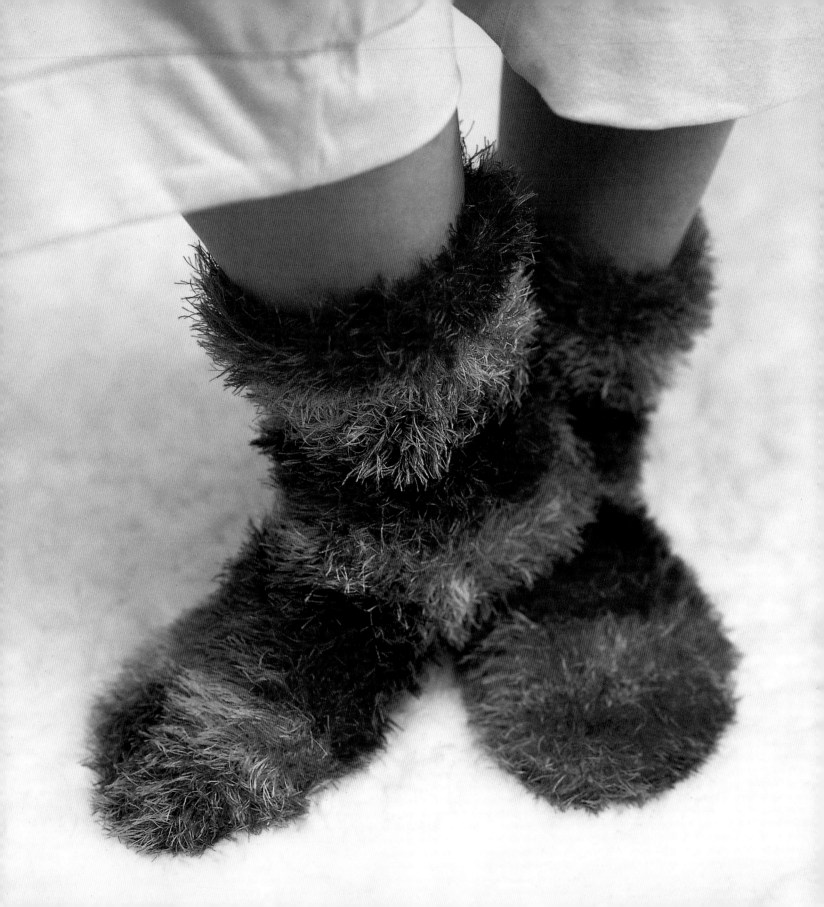

crazy **fur**

The small size of socks gives you a great opportunity to experiment with different yarns. You don't have to stick to sock yarns; this novelty yarn will create a light, furry pair of socks.

Sizes

CS (CM:CL:CXL:AS:AM:AL)

(See page 7.)

Materials

2 (2:2:2:3:3:4) 1¾ oz (50 g) balls of Scholler & Stahl La Ola Stripes

Color in rainbow/Clown 109

Set of US 3 (3.25 mm) double-pointed knitting needles

Gauge/Tension

24 sts and 34 rows to 4 in (10 cm) over stockinette/stocking stitch using US 3 (3.25 mm) needles.

Abbreviations

cm centimeter(s); **cont** continu(e)(ing); **g** gram(s); **in** inch(es); **k** knit; **mm** millimeter; **oz** ounce(s); **p** purl; **rep** repeat; **RS** right side; **st(s)** stitch(es); **wrap next st** wrap next stitch by slipping next stitch from left to right needle, take yarn to opposite side of work between needles, slip stitch back onto the left needle – when working wrapped stitches, work through both the stitch and the wrap.

Pattern note

When knitting a matching pair of socks using a self-patterning yarn, start the first sock at a color change. This makes it easy to identify the same place in the color sequence to start the second sock.

Socks (both alike)

Cast on 32 (36:40:44:48:52:56) sts.
Divide sts between 3 needles, join and place marker.

Rib

Working in the round:
Round 1 (RS) [K1, p1] to end.
Rep this last round 11 more times.

Cuff

Round 13 Knit.
Rep this last round until work measures
6¼ (7:7:8:8:8¾:8¾) in/16 (18:18:20:20:22:22) cm.

Heel shaping

*K7 (8:9:10:11:12:13), wrap next st, turn.
Row 1 P14 (16:18:20:22:24:26), wrap next st, turn.
Slide other 16 (18:20:22:24:26:28) sts (between wrapped sts) onto spare needles.
Row 2 K13 (15:17:19:21:23:25), wrap next st, turn.
Row 3 P12 (14:16:19:20:22:24), wrap next st, turn.
Cont in this way, working 1 less st before wrapping next st on each row until the following row has been worked:
P6 (6:6:8:8:8:8), wrap next st, turn.

Next row K6 (6:6:8:8:8:8), work wrapped st, wrap next st, turn.
Next row P7 (7:7:9:9:9:9), work wrapped st, wrap next st, turn.
Next row K8 (8:8:10:10:10:10), work double-wrapped st by knitting through the st and the two wraps together, wrap next st, turn.
Next row P9 (9:9:11:11:11:11), work double-wrapped st by purling through the st and the two wraps together, wrap next st, turn.

Cont in this way, working 1 more st before wrapping next st on each row until the following row has been worked:
P13 (15:17:19:21:23:25), work double-wrapped st, wrap next st, turn.*

Next row/round K14 (16:18:20:22:24:26), work double-wrapped st, knit across 16 (18:20:22:24:26:28) sts held on spare needles, work remaining double-wrapped st, k7 (8:9:10:11:12:13).

Foot

Knit 20 (24:28:32:40:48:56) rounds.

Toe shaping

Rep Heel shaping from * to *
Next row K14 (16:18:20:22:24:26), work double-wrapped st.
Graft sts from Foot and Toe sections using Kitchener stitch (see page 10), grafting the remaining wrapped st together with wraps.

Finishing

Sew in all ends.

the whole **hog**

When you put your feet together, these fun socks reveal a porky pig across your feet. The socks are worked flat then sewn up to create the matching pair.

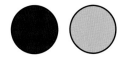

Sizes

CXL (AS:AM:AL:AXL)

(See page 7.)

Materials

1 (1:1:1:1) 3½ oz (100 g) balls of Opal Uni in main color M (brown/Chocolate 1411) and 1 (1:1:1:1) ball in A (pink/Pink 11)

Pair of US 2 (2.75 mm) knitting needles

Gauge/Tension

36 sts and 44 rows to 4 in (10 cm) over stockinette/stocking stitch using US 2 (2.75 mm) needles.

Abbreviations

cm centimeter(s); **cont** continu(e)(ing); **g** gram(s); **in** inch(es); **k** knit; **mm** millimeter; **oz** ounce(s); **p** purl; **rep** repeat; **RS** right side; **ssk2tog** [slip next stitch] twice, insert left needle into front of slipped stitches and knit together; **st(s)** stitch(es); **tog** together; **wrap next st** wrap next stitch by slipping next stitch from left to right needle, take yarn to opposite side of work between needles, slip stitch back onto the left needle – when working wrapped stitches, work through both the stitch and the wrap.

Left sock

*Using yarn M, cast on 114 (122:130:138:146) sts.
Row 1 (RS) K2tog, [p2tog, k2tog] to end.
57 (61:65:69:73) sts.

Rib
Row 2 P1, [k1, p1] to end.
Row 3 K1, [p1, k1] to end.
Rep these last two rows 6 more times.

Cuff
Work 45 rows from Chart A (see page 36).
Break off yarn A.
Using yarn M, work 15 rows.*

Heel shaping
Row 1 K55 (59:63:67:71), wrap next st, turn.

**Row 2 P26 (28:30:32:34), wrap next st, turn.
Row 3 K25 (27:29:31:33), wrap next st, turn.
Cont in this way, working 1 more st before wrapping next st on each row until the following row has been worked:
K9 (11:11:13:13), wrap next st, turn.

Next row P9 (11:11:13:13), work wrapped st, wrap next st, turn.
Next row K10 (12:12:14:14), work wrapped st, wrap next st, turn.
Next row P11 (13:13:15:15), work double-wrapped st by purling through the st and the two wraps together, wrap next st, turn.
Next row K12 (14:14:16:16), work double-wrapped st by knitting through the st and the two wraps together, wrap next st, turn.
Cont in this way, working 1 more st before wrapping next st on each row until the following row has been worked:

K26 (28:30:32:34) work double-wrapped st, wrap next st, turn.

Next row Purl to end, working the remaining double-wrapped st. 57 (61:65:69:73) sts.

Foot
Work 45 rows from Chart B (see page 37).
Break off yarn A.
Using yarn M, work 1 row.**

Toe shaping
Row 1 K1, [ssk2tog, k22 (24:26:28:30), k2tog, k2] twice. 53 (57:61:65:69) sts.
Row 2 Purl.
Row 3 K1, [ssk2tog, k20 (22:24:26:28), k2tog, k2] twice. 49 (53:57:61:65) sts.
Row 4 Purl.
Cont decreasing in this way until 21(25:25:29:29) sts remain.
Next row P2tog, p9 (11:11:13:13), so ending halfway across the row.
See Finishing.

Right sock
Work as for Left sock from * to *.

Heel shaping
Row 1 K28 (30:32:34:36), wrap next st, turn.
Work as for Left sock from ** to **.

Toe shaping
Row 1 [K2, ssk2tog, k22 (24:26:28:30), k2tog] twice, k1. 53 (57:61:65:69) sts.
Row 2 Purl.
Row 3 [K2, ssk2tog, k20 (22:24:26:28), k2tog] twice, k1. 49 (53:57:61:65) sts.
Row 4 Purl.

The whole hog socks chart A

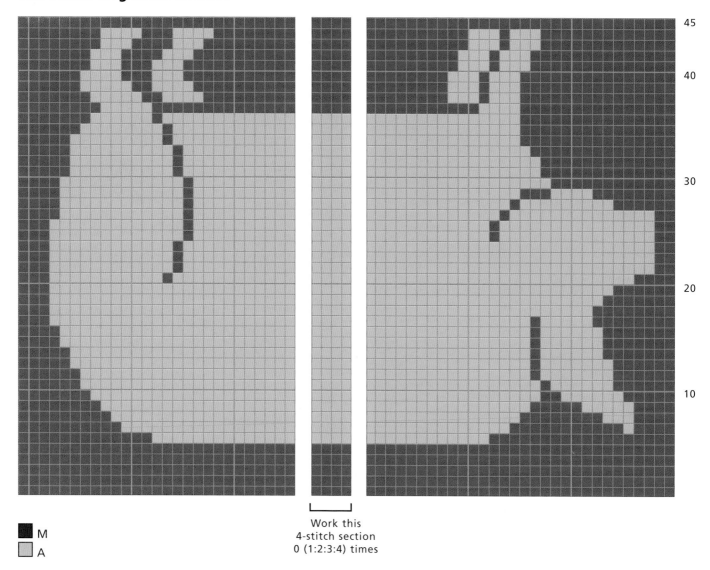

45
40
30
20
10

■ M
☐ A

Work this
4-stitch section
0 (1:2:3:4) times

Cont decreasing in this way until 25 (29:29:33:33) sts remain.

Next row Purl.

Next row K2tog, ssk2tog, k6 (8:8:10:10), k2tog, k2, ssktog, k6 (8:8:10:10), k2tog, k1. 20 (24:24:28:28) sts.

Next row P10 (12:12:14:14), so ending halfway across the row.

Finishing

Graft remaining toe sts together using Kitchener stitch (see page 10).

Join side seam, taking half a stitch into seam from each edge. Secure end of yarn inside sock. Embroider stem stitch tails and French-knot eyes onto pigs as in photograph.

The whole hog socks chart B

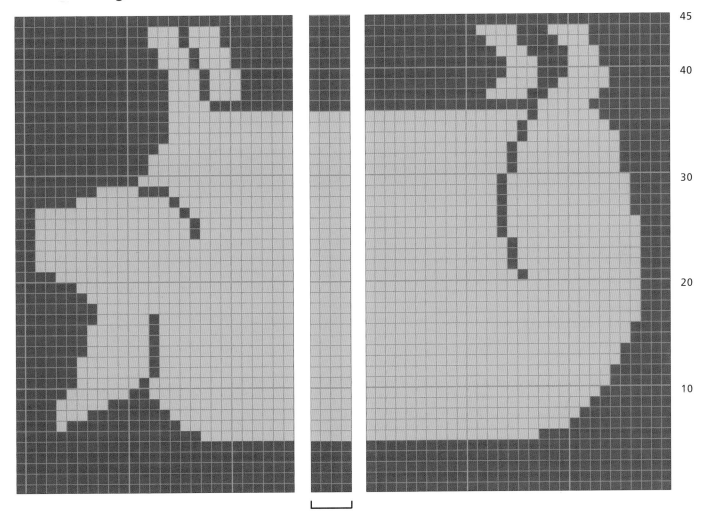

Work this
4-stitch section
0 (1:2:3:4) times

45

40

30

20

10

rainbow **toes**

These socks are not only fun to knit, they are also warm and cozy to wear as each toe gets its own individual woolly coat. Peep-toe shoes will show off your rainbow toes to the world.

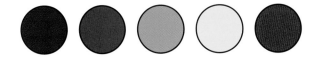

Sizes
CXL (AS:AM:AL)
(See page 7.)

Materials
1 (1:1:2) 3½ oz (100 g) balls of Opal Uni in main color M (red/Red 10) and 1 (1:1:1:1) ball each of A (blue/Blue 26), B (green/Green 40), C (yellow/Yellow 03) and D (purple/Purple 18)
Set of US 2 (2.75 mm) double-pointed knitting needles

Gauge/Tension
36 sts and 44 rows to 4 in (10 cm) over stockinette/stocking stitch using US 2 (2.75 mm) needles

Abbreviations
cm centimeter(s); **cont** continu(e)(ing); **dec** decreas(e)(ing); **g** gram(s); **in** inch(es); **k** knit; **mm** millimeter; **oz** ounce(s); **p** purl; **rep** repeat; **RS** right side; **ssk2tog** [slip next stitch] twice, insert left needle into front of slipped stitches and knit together; **st(s)** stitch(es); **tog** together; **wrap next st** wrap next stitch by slipping next stitch from left to right needle, take yarn to opposite side of work between needles, slip stitch back onto the left needle – when working wrapped stitches, work through both the stitch and the wrap.

Left sock

*Using yarn D, cast on 84 (90:94:100) sts.
Divide sts between 3 needles, join and place marker.

Rib

Working in the round:
Round 1 (RS) [K1, p1] to end.
Cont in rib as set, working 2 rounds in yarn A, 2 in yarn B, 2 in yarn C.
Change to yarn M and cont in rib until work measures 4¾ in (12 cm).

Cuff

Next round Knit.
Rep this last round until work measures 5½ in (14 cm).
Dec round K2, k2tog, k to last 4 sts, ssk2tog, k2. 82 (88:92:98) sts.
Knit 4 rounds.
Rep these last 5 rounds until 56 (60:64:68) sts remain.
Next round Knit.
Rep this last round until work measures 15¾ (18:19:19½) in/40 (46:48:50) cm.

Heel shaping

K13 (14:15:16), wrap next st, turn.
Row 1 P26 (28:30:32), wrap next st, turn.
Slide other 28 (30:32:34) sts (sts between wrapped sts) onto spare needles.
Row 2 K25 (27:29:31), wrap next st, turn.
Row 3 P24 (26:28:30), wrap next st, turn.
Cont in this way, working 1 more st before wrapping next st on each row until the following row has been worked:
P12, wrap next st, turn.

Next row K12, work wrapped st, wrap next st, turn.
Next row P13, work wrapped st, wrap next st, turn.
Next row K14, work double-wrapped st by knitting through the st and the two wraps together, wrap next st, turn.

Next row P15, work double-wrapped st by purling through the st and the two wraps together, wrap next st, turn.
Cont in this way, working 1 more st before wrapping next st on each row until the following row has been worked:
P25 (27:29:31), work double-wrapped st, wrap next st, turn.

Next row/round K26 (28:30:32), work double-wrapped st, k28 (30:32:34) sts held on spare needles, work remaining double-wrapped st, k13 (14:15:16).

Foot

Next round Knit.
Rep this last round until work measures 6¼ (7:7¾:8¾) in/16 (18:20:22) cm from back of Heel.*
K14 (15:16:17) and move marker indicating beginning and ends of rounds to this point.

**Toes

Little toe
Knit 22 (24:26:28), change to yarn D (do not break yarn M), k12, cast on 3 sts.

Redistribute the 15 sts in yarn D onto 3 needles and leave remaining sts on spare needles.
Working in the round:
On the 15 sts, knit until toe measures 1 in (2.5 cm).
Next round K1, [k2tog] to end. 8 sts.
Break yarn, thread through sts and draw up tightly.

Fourth toe
Using yarn M, pick up and knit 4 sts from those cast on in yarn D, knit to marker. 48 (52:56:60) sts.
Knit 1 round.
Next round K18 (19:21:22), change to yarn A (do not break yarn M), k12 (14:14:16), cast on 3 sts.
Redistribute the 15 (17:17:19) sts in yarn A onto 3

needles and leave remaining sts on spare needles. Working in the round: on the 15 (17:17:19) sts knit until toe measures 1¼ in (3 cm).

Next round K1, [k2tog] to end. 8 (9:9:10) sts.
Break yarn, thread through sts and draw up tightly.

Third toe

Using yarn M, pick up and knit 4 sts from those cast on in yarn A, knit to marker. 40 (42:46:48) sts.
Knit 1 round.

Next round K13 (14:16:16), change to yarn B (do not break yarn M), k14 (14:14:16), cast on 3 sts.
Redistribute the 17 (17:17:19) sts in yarn B onto 3 needles and leave remaining sts on spare needles. Working in the round: on the 17 (17:17:19) sts knit until toe measures 1¼ in (3 cm).

Next round K1, [k2tog] to end. 9 (9:9:10) sts.
Break yarn, thread through sts and draw up tightly.

Second toe

Using yarn M, pick up and knit 4 sts from those cast on in yarn B, knit to marker. 30 (32:36:36) sts.
Knit 1 round.

Next round K8(9:10:10), change to yarn C (do not break yarn M), k14 (14:16:16), cast on 3 sts.
Redistribute the 17 (17:19:19) sts in yarn C onto 3 needles and leave remaining sts on spare needles. Working in the round: on the 17 (17:19:19) sts knit until toe measures 1¼ in (3 cm).

Next round K1, [k2tog] to end. 9 (9:10:10) sts.
Break yarn, thread through sts and draw up tightly.

Big toe

Using yarn M pick up and knit 4 sts from those cast on in yarn C, knit to marker. 20 (22:24:24) sts. Working in the round knit until toe measures 1¼ in (3 cm).

Next round K2 (1:0:0), [k2tog, k1] to end.
14 (15:16:16) sts.

Next round K0 (1:0:0), [k2tog] to end. 7 (8:8:8) sts.
Break yarn, thread through sts and draw up tightly.**

Right sock

Work as for Left sock from * to *.
K42 (45:48:51) and move marker indicating beginning and ends of rounds to this point.
Work as for Left sock from ** to ** to complete.

Finishing

Sew in all ends.

thigh **highs**

Knitted in a stretchy yarn and a lacy pattern, these socks are ideal for those who want to show off their shapely legs. Choose a yarn color to suit your skin tone: dark colors for pale skin and vice versa works well.

Size

AS

(See page 7.)

Materials

2 3½oz (100 g) balls of Schoeller & Stahl Fortissima Socka Stretch 100 in brown/Dark Brown 82

Set each of US 2 (2.75 mm) and US 4 (3.5 mm) double-pointed knitting needles

Gauge/Tension

22 sts and 36 rows to 4 in (10 cm) over lace patt using US 4 (3.5 mm) needles

Abbreviations

beg beginning; **cm** centimeter(s); **cont** continu(e)(ing); **dec** decreas(e)(ing); **foll** following; **g** gram(s); **in** inch(es); **k** knit; **M1** make one by inserting left needle under strand between needles and working into the back of it; **mm** millimeter; **oz** ounce(s); **p** purl; **patt** pattern; **psso** pass slipped stitch over; **rep** repeat; **RS** right side; **sl1** slip one stitch; **ssk2tog** [slip next stitch] twice, insert left needle into front of slipped stitches and knit together; **st(s)** stitch(es); **tog** together; **wrap next st** wrap next stitch by slipping next stitch from left to right needle, take yarn to opposite side of work between needles, slip stitch back onto the left needle – when working wrapped stitches, work through both the stitch and the wrap; **yf** yarn forward.

Socks (both alike)

Using US 2 (2.75 mm) needles, cast on 284 sts.
Divide sts between 3 needles, join and place marker.
Working in the round:

Round 1 (RS) [K2tog] twice, *[p2tog] twice, [k2tog] twice, rep from * to end. 142 sts.

Round 2 K2, [p2, k2] rep to end.

Rep this last round 17 more times.

Change to US 4 (3.5 mm) needles

Round 20 K1, [k2tog, k1] to end. 95 sts.

Round 21 K2, *yf, sl1, k2tog, psso, yf, k1, rep from * to last st, k1.

Round 22 Knit.

Round 23 K1, k2tog, yf, k1, *yf, sl1, k2tog, psso, yf, k1, rep from * to last 3 sts, yf, sl1, k1, psso, k1.

Round 24 Knit.

Last 4 rounds form patt.

Keeping patt correct, work 3 rounds.

Next round K1, k2tog, k to last 3 sts, ssk2tog, k1.

Working all decreases as set by last round and keeping patt correct, dec 1 st at beg and end of 4th and every foll 4th round until 51 sts remain.

Cont straight until work measures 24 in (60 cm), ending after patt round 22 or 24.

Heel shaping

Change to US 2 (2.75 mm) needles.

K11, wrap next st, turn.

Row 1 P1, [M1, p4] 5 times, M1, p1, wrap next st, turn.

Slide other 27 sts (between wrapped sts) onto spare needles.

Row 2 K27, wrap next st, turn.

Row 3 P26, wrap next st, turn.

Cont in this way, working 1 more st before wrapping next st on each row until the foll row has been worked:
P12, wrap next st, turn.

Next row K12, work wrapped st, wrap next st, turn.

Next row P13, work wrapped st, wrap next st, turn.

Next row K14, work double-wrapped st by knitting through the st and the two wraps together, wrap next st, turn.

Next row P15, work double-wrapped st by purling through the st and the two wraps together, wrap next st, turn.

Cont in this way, working 1 more st before wrapping next st on each row until the foll row has been worked:
P27, work double-wrapped st, wrap next st, turn.

Next row/round K28, work double-wrapped st, change to US 4 (3.5 mm) needles and patt across 27 sts held on spare needles, work remaining double-wrapped st, k1, [k2tog, k3] twice, k2tog, k1.

Foot

Next round K2, [k2tog, k3] twice, k2tog, patt to end. 51 sts.

Cont straight in patt until work measures 7 in (18 cm) from back of heel, ending after patt round 22 or 24.
Change to US 2 (2.75 mm) needles.

Next round K6, M1, k5, M1, [k6, M1] twice, k5, M1, [k6, M1] twice, k5, M1 k6, M1. 60 sts.

Decrease for toe

Place markers after the 15th and 45th sts.

Round 1 Knit to 3 sts before first marker, k2tog, k1 (marker), k1, ssk2tog, knit to 3 sts before next marker, k2tog, k1 (marker), k1, ssk2tog, knit to end.

Round 2 Knit.

Rep these last two rounds until 24 sts remain.
Knit to first marker.

Rearrange sts so that the first 6 and last 6 sts of the round are on one needle with the 12 middle sts on another needle.
Graft toe together using Kitchener stitch (see page 10).

Finishing

Sew in all ends.

zigzag **socks**

These might look complicated but using a simple stitch pattern and a self-patterning yarn it is easy to create this dynamic zigzag effect. The design works best with a boldly colored yarn.

Sizes

CXL (AS:AM:AL:AXL)

(See page 7.)

Materials

1 (1:1:2:2) 1¾ oz (50 g) balls of Regia Mini Ringels in blue-multi stripes/Royal 5219

Set of US 2 (2.75 mm) double-pointed knitting needles

Gauge/Tension

36 sts and 44 rows to 4 in (10 cm) over stockinette/stocking stitch using US 2 (2.75 mm) needles

Abbreviations

cm centimeter(s); **cont** continu(e)(ing); **g** gram(s); **in** inch(es); **k** knit; **M1** make one by inserting left needle under strand between needles and working into the back of it; **mm** millimeter; **oz** ounce(s); **p** purl; **patt** pattern; **rep** repeat; **RS** right side; **ssk2tog** [slip next stitch] twice, insert left needle into front of slipped stitches and knit together; **st(s)** stitch(es); **tog** together.

Pattern note

When knitting a matching pair of socks using a self-patterning yarn, start the first sock at a color change. This makes it easy to identify the same place in the color sequence to start the second sock.

Socks (both alike)

Cast on 60 (64:68:72:76) sts.
Divide sts between 3 needles, join and place marker.

Cuff

Working in the round:
Round 1 (RS) Knit.
Round 2 Purl.
Rep these last two rounds once more.
Round 5 Knit.
Round 6 *Ssk2tog, k5 (5:6:6:7), M1, k1, M1,
k5 (6:6:7:7), k2tog, rep from * to end.
Last two rounds form patt.
Cont in patt until work measures 8 (8¼:8½:9) in/20
(21:22:23:24) cm.

Heel flap

Patt 15 (16:17:18:19), turn.
Row 1 30 (32:34:36:38), turn.
Slide other 30 (32:34:36:38) sts onto spare needles.
Row 2 [Ssk2tog, k11(12:13:14:15), k2tog] twice, turn.
26 (28:30:32:34) sts.
Working back and forth on these 26 (28:30:32:34) sts,
cont as follows:
Row 3 Purl.
Row 4 Knit.
Rep these last two rows 9 (11:13:15:17) more times.

Heel shaping

Row 1 Sl1, p14 (15:16:17:18), p2tog, p1, turn.
Row 2 Sl1, k5, ssk2tog, k1, turn.
Row 3 Sl1, p6, p2tog, p1, turn.
Row 4 Sl1, k7, ssk2tog, k1, turn.
Cont in this way, taking one more stitch in each row
until the row 'Sl1, k13 (13:15:15:17), ssk2tog, k1, turn'
has been worked. (For CXL, AM and AXL, do NOT turn
at end of this last row.)
AS, AL only:
Next row Sl1, p-(14:-:16:-), p2tog, turn.

Next row Sl1, k-(14:-:16:-), ssk2tog.
All sizes: 16 (16:18:18:20) sts.

Pick up for instep

Pick up knitwise 13 (14:15:16:17) sts down side of heel
flap, place marker.
Patt 30 (32:34:36:38) sts from cuff, place marker, pick up
knitwise 13 (14:15:16:17) sts up side of heel flap,
k8 (8:9:9:10). 74 (78:84:88:96) sts.

Shape instep

Round 1 Knit to 3 sts before first marker, k2tog, k1
(marker), patt 30 (32:34:36:38) (marker), k1, ssk2tog, knit
to end. 70 (74:82:84:92) sts.
Round 2 K to first marker, patt to next marker, k to end.
Rep these last two rounds until 56 (60:64:68:72) sts remain.

Foot

Keeping patt panel as set on top of foot, patt
31 (34:37:40:43) rounds.

Decrease for toe

Round 1 K13 (14:15:16:17), *ssk2tog, k11 (12:13:14:15),
k2tog, rep from * once more, k13 (14:15:16:17).
52 (56:60:64:68) sts.
Round 2 Knit to 3 sts before first marker, k2tog, k1
(marker), k1, ssk2tog, knit to 3 sts before next marker, k2tog,
k1 (marker), k1, ssk2tog, knit to end. 48 (52:56:60:64) sts.
Round 3 Knit.
Rep these last two rounds until 24 sts remain.
Knit to first marker.

Rearrange sts so that the first 6 and last 6 sts of the round
are on one needle with the 12 middle sts on another.
Graft toe together using Kitchener stitch (see page 10).

Finishing

Sew in all ends.

sock **buddies**

These great socks have little pockets on the sides to keep treasures safe. Knit the little teddies, too, and the wearer will never be far away from their best friends.

Sizes

CS (CM:CL:CXL)

(See page 7.)

Materials

2 (2:2:2) 1¾ oz (50 g) balls of Regia Silk 6-ply in main color M (stone/Linen 005), 1 (1:1:1) ball in A (brown/Mocha 10) and oddment of black yarn for embroidery

Pair of US 2½ (3 mm) knitting needles

Set of US 3 (3.25 mm) double-pointed knitting needles

Small amount toy filling

Gauge/Tension

24 sts and 34 rows to 4 in (10 cm) over stockinette/stocking stitch using US 3 (3.25 mm) needles

Abbreviations

cm centimeter(s); **cont** continu(e)(ing); **in** inch(es); **g** gram(s); **k** knit; **mm** millimeter; **oz** ounce(s); **p** purl; **rep** repeat; **RS** right side; **sl1** slip one stitch; **ssk2tog** [slip next stitch] twice, insert left needle into front of slipped stitches and knit together; **st(s)** stitch(es); **tog** together.

Left sock

**Using US 3 (3.25 mm) double-pointed needles and yarn M, cast on 32 (36:40:44) sts.
Divide sts between 3 needles, join and place marker.

Rib

Working in the round:
Round 1 (RS) *K2, p2, rep from * to end.
Rep this last round 23 more times.

Cuff

Knit 10 rounds.**

Place pocket
Round 35 K29 (32:35:38), turn.
Pocket lining
Next row P10, turn.
Working on these 10 sts only (leaving others on spare needles), work 15 rows in stockinette/stocking stitch. Cast off.
Return to remaining sts and rejoin yarn.
Cast on 10 sts over those used for Pocket Lining and knit to end of round.
Round 36 K19 (22:25:28), [p2, k2] twice, p2, knit to end.
Rep this last round 14 more times.

***Next round** Knit.
Rep this last round until work measures 7¾ (8½:9¼:9¾) in/20 (22:24:25) cm.

Heel flap

K8 (9:10:11), turn.
Row 1 Sl1, p15 (17:19:21), turn.
Slide other 16 (18:20:22) sts onto spare needles.
Row 2 Sl1, k15 (17:19:21), turn.
Working back and forth on these 16 (18:20:22) sts, rep these last two rows 7 (8:9:10) more times.

Heel shaping

Row 1 Sl1, p9 (10:11:12), p2tog, p1, turn.
Row 2 Sl1, k5, ssk2tog, k1, turn.
Row 3 Sl1, p6, p2tog, p1, turn.
Row 4 Sl1, k7, ssk2tog, k1, turn.
Cont in this way, taking one more stitch in each row, for a further 0 (2:2:4) rows. (For CM and CXL, do NOT turn at end of last of these rows.)
CS, CL only:
Next row Sl1, p8 (-:10:-) p2tog, turn.
Next row Sl1, k8 (-:10:-), ssk2tog.
All sizes: 10 (12:12:14) sts.

Pick up for instep

Pick up knitwise 8 (9:10:11) sts down side of heel flap, place marker,
knit 16 (18:20:22) sts from cuff, place marker,
pick up knitwise 8 (9:10:11) sts up side of heel flap,
k5 (6:6:7). 42 (48:52:58) sts.

Shape instep

Round 1 Knit to 3 sts before first marker, k2tog, k1 (marker), knit to next marker (marker), k1, ssk2tog, knit to end. 40 (46:50:56) sts.
Round 2 Knit.
Rep these last two rounds until 32 (36:40:44) sts remain.

Foot

Knit 20 (24:28:32) rounds.

Decrease for toe

Round 1 Knit to 3 sts before first marker, k2tog, k1 (marker), k1, ssk2tog, knit to 3 sts before next marker, k2tog, k1 (marker), k1, ssk2tog, knit to end. 28 (34:36:40) sts.
Round 2 Knit.
Rep these last two rounds until 16 sts remain.
Knit to first marker.

Rearrange sts so that the first 4 and last 4 sts of the round are on one needle with the 8 middle sts on another needle.
Graft toe together using Kitchener stitch (see page 10).***

Right sock

Work as for Left sock from ** to **.

Place pocket
Round 35 K13(14:15:16), turn.
Pocket lining
Next row P10, turn.
Working on these 10 sts only (leaving others on spare needles), work 15 rows in stockinette/stocking stitch. Cast off.
Return to remaining sts and rejoin yarn.
Cast on 10 sts over those used for Pocket lining and knit to end of round.
Round 36 K3 (4:5:6), [p2, k2] twice, p2, knit to end.
Rep this last round 14 more times.

Work as for Left sock from *** to *** to complete.

Finishing

Sew in all ends.

Teddies
(make 2)

Head and Body
Using US 2½ (3 mm) needles and yarn A, cast on 22 sts.
Work in stockinette/stocking stitch until work measures 3¼ in (8 cm).
Cast off.

Arms
(make 2 for each Teddy)
Using US 2½ (3 mm) needles and yarn A, cast on 8 sts.
Work in stockinette/stocking stitch until work measures 1¼ in (3 cm).
Cast off.

Making up
Fold Head and Body in half lengthwise. Join sides of work and cast-off edge.
Stuff lightly with toy filling and close base seam (cast-on edge).
Using yarn A and photograph as a guide, gather tightly around neck to shape head. Sew a line of running stitch from cast-on edge one third of way up body section to define legs. Gather tightly around each 'corner' of cast-off edge to form ears.
Embroider face using black yarn.
Fold each Arm in half lengthwise. Join sides of work and cast-on edge. Stuff lightly with toy filling and close top (cast-off) edge. Using photograph as a guide, attach Arms to Body.

Finishing
Sew in all ends. If desired, attach teddies to inside of pocket with a short length of cord or plaited yarn.

fly away **home**

These little ladybugs look so cute on tiny toes. The bold spots and contrast colors are great for little babies and the socks are so small that the pattern is quick to knit.

Sizes
To fit
0–3 (3–6:6–12) months

Materials
2 (2:2) 1¾ oz (50 g) balls of Schoeller & Stahl Fortissima in main color M (red/Geranium 1010), 1 (1:1) ball in A (black/Black 1024) and a piece of white yarn for embroidery.
Set of US 2 (2.75 mm) double-pointed knitting needles

Gauge/Tension
36 sts and 44 rows to 4 in (10 cm) over stockinette/stocking stitch using US 2 (2.75 mm) needles

Abbreviations
cm centimeter(s); **g** gram(s); **in** inch(es); **k** knit; **mm** millimeter; **oz** ounce(s); **p** purl; **rep** repeat; **ssk2tog** [slip next stitch] twice, insert left needle into front of slipped stitches and knit together; **st(s)** stitch(es); **tog** together; **wrap next st** wrap next stitch by slipping next stitch from left to right needle, take yarn to opposite side of work between needles, slip stitch back onto the left needle – when working wrapped stitches, work through both the stitch and the wrap; **WS** wrong side.

Socks (both alike)

Using yarn A, cast on 44 (48:48) sts.
Divide sts between 3 needles, join and place marker.

Cuff

Working in the round:
Change to yarn M.
Round 1 *K1, p1, rep from * to end.
Rep this last round 24 (24:29) more times.

Heel shaping

Knit 1 round.
Row 1 K10 (11:11), wrap next st, turn.
Row 2 P20 (22:22), wrap next st, turn.
Slide other 22 (24:24) sts (between wrapped sts) on to spare needles.
Row 3 K19 (21:21), wrap next st, turn.
Row 4 P18 (20:20), wrap next st, turn.
Working back and forth on these sts, rep the last two rows, working 1 less st each time before wrapping next st until the following row has been worked:
P4 (6:6), wrap next st, turn.

Next row K4 (6:6), K the wrapped st (by knitting together the stitch and the loop around it), turn.
Next row P5 (7:7), P the wrapped st (by purling together the stitch and the loop around it), turn.
Rep the last two rows, working 1 more stitch each time, until all the wrapped stitches have been worked, ending on a WS row.
22 (24:24) sts.
Turn and knit to marker.

Foot

Next round K11 (12:12), place marker, k22 (24:24) sts held on spare needles, place marker, k11 (12:12). Three markers in total now placed.
K12 (15:18) rounds.

Decrease for toe

Change to yarn A.
Round 1 Knit to 3 sts before first marker, k2tog, k1 (1st marker), k1, ssk2tog, knit to 3 sts before next marker, k2tog, k1 (2nd marker), k1, ssk2tog, knit to end (original marker).
40 (44:44) sts.
Rep this last round until 8 sts remain.
Knit to first marker.

Rearrange sts so that the first 2 and last 2 sts of the round are on one needle with the 4 middle sts on another needle.
Graft toe together using Kitchener stitch (see page 10).

Finishing

Sew in all ends.
Using yarn A, embroider a line of backstitch down the center of the top of the foot. Using Chart and photograph as a guide, Swiss-darn spots in yarn A. Using white yarn, embroider backstitch eyes on black toe section.

Fly away home socks chart

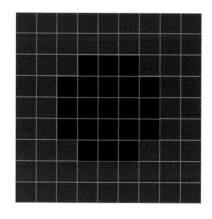

 M
A

cozy **toes**

covered **in cable**

Cable patterns not only add interest to your socks, they also make for thicker, warmer, stretchier socks. And, as the cables give the fabric more body, a ribbed cuff isn't required, great if you don't like your socks tight around your ankles.

Sizes
CL–CXL (AS–AM:AL)
(See page 7.)

Materials
1 (1:1) 3½ oz (100 g) ball of Opal Uni in main color M (green/Green 40) and 1 (1:1) ball in A (orange/Orange 06)
Set of US 2 (2.75 mm) double-pointed knitting needles
Cable needle

Gauge/Tension
36 sts and 44 rows to 4 in (10 cm) over stockinette/stocking stitch using US 2 (2.75 mm) needles

Abbreviations
cm centimeter(s); **cont** continu(e)(ing); **C10B** slip next five stitches onto cable needle and hold at back of work, knit next five stitches from left-hand needle then knit five stitches from cable needle; **C10F** slip next five stitches onto cable needle and hold at front of work, knit next five stitches from left-hand needle then knit five stitches from cable needle; **g** gram(s); **in** inch(es); **k** knit; **mm** millimeter; **oz** ounce(s); **p** purl; **patt** pattern; **psso** pass slipped stitch over; **rep** repeat; **RS** right side; **sl1** slip one stitch; **ssk2tog** [slip next stitch] twice, insert left needle into front of slipped stitches and knit together; **st(s)** stitch(es); **tog** together.

Cable pattern
Rounds 1–2 Knit.
Round 3 (RS) *C10F, k5, rep from * to end.
Rounds 4–8 Knit.
Round 9 *C10B, k5, rep from * to end.
Rounds 10–12 Knit.
Rep these 12 rounds.

Socks (both alike)
Using yarn A, cast on 105 (120:135) sts.
Divide sts between 3 needles, join and place marker.

Cuff
Round 1 Knit.
Round 2 Purl.
Rep these two rounds once. Change to yarn M.
Begin cable patt and cont straight until work measures
approximately 7 (8:9) in/18 (20:23) cm, ending with a
round 11.
Next round [K2tog] 13 (15:17) times, k53 (60:67),
[k2tog] 13 (15:17) times. 79 (90:101) sts.

Heel flap
K13 (15:17), turn.
Change to yarn A.
Row 1 Sl1, p25 (29:33), turn.
Slide other 53 (60:67) sts onto spare needles.
Row 2 Sl1, k25 (29:33), turn.
Working back and forth on these 26 (30:34) sts, rep
these last two rows 10 (14:18) more times.

Heel shaping
Row 1 Sl1, p14 (16:18), p2tog, p1, turn.
Row 2 Sl1, k5, ssk2tog, k1, turn.
Row 3 Sl1, p6, p2tog, p1, turn.
Row 4 Sl1, k7, ssk2tog, k1, turn.
Cont in this way, taking in 1 more st each row until all
the heel flap sts have been included, ending with a RS
row. Do NOT turn at end of this last row. 16 (18:20) sts.

Pick up for instep
Change to yarn M.
Pick up knitwise 13 (15:17) sts down side of heel flap,
place marker.
Knit 53 (60:67) sts from cuff, place marker,
pick up knitwise 13(15:17) sts up side of heel flap,
k8 (9:10). 95 (108:121) sts.

Shape instep
Round 1 Knit to 3 sts before first marker, k2tog, k1
(marker), patt to next marker (marker), k1, ssk2tog, knit to
end. 93 (106:119) sts.
Round 2 Knit to first marker, patt to next, knit to end.
Rep these last two rounds until 79 (90:101) sts remain.

Foot
Cont straight as set until work measures approximately
6¼ (7:8) in/16 (18:20) cm from back of heel, ending with a
patt round 5 or 11.
Next round Knit to first marker, [k2tog] 12 (30:16) times,
[sl1, k2tog, psso] 1 (0:0) times, k0 (0:1), [k2tog] 13 (0:17)
times, knit to end. 52 (60:68) sts.

Decrease for toe
Change to yarn A.
Round 1 Knit to 3 sts before first marker, k2tog, k1
(marker), k1, ssk2tog, knit to 3 sts before next marker,
k2tog, k1 (marker), k1, ssk2tog, knit to end. 48 (56:64) sts.
Round 2 Knit.
Rep these last two rounds until 24 sts remain.
Knit to first marker.

Rearrange sts so that the first 6 and last 6 sts of the round
are on one needle with the 12 middle sts on another.
Graft toe together using Kitchener stitch (see page 10).

Finishing
Sew in all ends.

frilled **to meet you**

Add some flirty frills to your socks with a soft, fluffy mohair yarn. The frills are worked separately and then knitted into your socks as you work the pattern.

Sizes

CM (CL:CXL:AS:AM:AL)

(See page 7.)

Materials

1 (2:2:2:2:2) 3¾ oz (110 g) hanks of Colinette Jitterbug in main color M (white-pink/Marble 88) and 1 (2:2:2:2:2) ¾ oz (25 g) hanks of Colinette Parisienne in A (white-pink/Marble 88)

US 2 (2.75 mm) circular knitting needle

Set of US 2 (2.75 mm) double-pointed knitting needles

Gauge/Tension

36 sts and 44 rows to 4 in (10 cm) over stockinette/stocking stitch using US 2 (2.75 mm) needles and yarn M

Abbreviations

cm centimeter(s); **cont** continu(e)(ing); **g** gram(s); **in** inch(es); **k** knit; **mm** millimeter; **oz** ounce(s); **p** purl; **rep** repeat; **RS** right side; **sl1** slip one stitch; **ssk2tog** [slip next stitch] twice, insert left needle into front of slipped stitches and knit together; **st(s)** stitch(es); **tog** together.

Frills

(make 10 (12:12:12:12:14))

Make and leave on needle until required.

Using US 2 (2.75 mm) circular needle and yarn A, cast on 392 (424:456:488:520:552) sts.

Row 1 Knit.

Row 2 [K2tog] to end. 196 (212:228:244:260:276) sts.

Row 3 [K2tog] to end. 98 (106:114:122:130:138) sts.

Row 4 [K2tog] to end. 49 (53:57:61:65:69) sts.

Socks (both alike)

Using US 2 (2.75 mm) double-pointed needles and yarn M, cast on 48 (52:56:60:64:68) sts.

Divide sts between 3 needles, join and place marker.

Rib

Working in the round:

Round 1 (RS) [K1, p1] to end.

Rep this last round 11 more times.

Cuff

Rounds 13 and 14 Knit.

**Round 15 Hold first Frill at right side of work and knit together one Frill st with each Cuff st, then knit last Frill st together with first st of next round.

Knit 7 (8:8:8:8:9) rounds.

Rep from **4 (5:5:5:5:6) more times.

Knit 2 rounds.

Heel flap

K12 (13:14:15:16:17), turn.

Row 1 Sl1, p23 (25:27:29:31:33), turn.

Slide other 24 (26:28:30:32:34) sts onto spare needles.

Row 2 Sl1, k23 (25:27:29:31:33), turn.

Working back and forth on these 24 (26:28:30:32:34) sts, rep these last two rows 8 (10:12:14:16:18) more times.

Heel shaping

Row 1 Sl1, p13 (14:15:16:17:18), p2tog, p1, turn.

Row 2 Sl1, k5, ssk2tog, k1, turn.

Row 3 Sl1, p6, p2tog, p1, turn.

Row 4 Sl1, k7, ssk2tog, k1, turn.

Cont in this way, taking one more stitch in each row until the row 'Sl1, k11(13:13:15:15:17), ssktog, k1, turn' has been worked. (For CL, AS and AL, do NOT turn at end of last of these rows.)

CM, CXL, AM only:

Next row Sl1, p12 (-:14:-:16:-) p2tog, turn.

Next row Sl1, k12 (-:14:-:16:-), ssk2tog.

All sizes: 14 (16:16:18:18:20) sts.

Pick up for instep

Pick up knitwise 12 (13:14:15:16:17) sts down side of heel flap, place marker,

knit 24 (26:28:30:32:34) sts from cuff, place marker, pick up knitwise 12 (13:14:15:16:17) sts up side of heel flap,

k7 (8:8:9:9:10). 62 (68:72:78:82:88) sts.

Shape instep

Round 1 Knit to 3 sts before first marker, k2tog, k1 (marker), knit to next marker, k1, ssk2tog, knit to end. 60 (66:70:76:80:86) sts.

Round 2 Knit.

Rep these last two rounds until 48 (52:56:60:64:68) sts remain.

Foot

Knit 36 (39:42:45:48:51) rounds.

Decrease for toe

Round 1 Knit to 3 sts before first marker, k2tog, k1 (marker), k1, ssk2tog, knit to 3 sts before next marker, k2tog, k1 (marker), k1, ssk2tog, knit to end. 44 (48:52:56:60:64) sts.

Round 2 Knit.
Rep these last two rounds until 24 sts remain.
Knit to first marker.

Rearrange sts so that the first 6 and last 6 sts of the
round are on one needle with the 12 middle sts on
another needle.
Graft toe together using Kitchener stitch (see page 10).

Finishing
Sew in all ends.

fab **for flip flops**

A special pair of socks designed especially with a separate big toe for wearing with flip flops. The self-patterning yarn is perfect as so much of the sock will be on show.

Sizes
CXL (AS:AM:AL:AXL)
(See page 7.)

Materials
1 (2:2:2:2) 1¾ oz (50 g) balls of Regia Jacquard in blue-beige/Tundra 5273
Set of US 2 (2.75 mm) double-pointed knitting needles

Gauge/Tension
36 sts and 44 rows to 4 in (10 cm) over stockinette/stocking stitch using US 2 (2.75 mm) needles

Abbreviations
cm centimeter(s); **cont** continu(e)(ing); **g** gram(s); **in** inch(es); **k** knit; **mm** millimeter; **oz** ounce(s); **p** purl; **rem** remaining; **rep** repeat; **RS** right side; **sl1** slip one stitch; **ssk2tog** [slip next stitch] twice, insert left needle into front of slipped stitches and knit together; **st(s)** stitch(es); **tog** together.

Pattern note
When knitting a matching pair of socks using a self-patterning yarn, start the first sock at a color change. This makes it easy to identify the same place in the color sequence to start the second sock.

Left sock

Cast on 56 (60:64:68:72) sts.
Divide sts between 3 needles, join and place marker.

Rib

Working in the round:
**Knit 3 rounds.
Round 4 *K1, p1, rep from * to end.
Rep this last round 14 more times.

Cuff

Knit 56 (60:64:68:72) rounds.

Heel flap

K14 (15:16:17:18), turn.
Row 1 Sl1, p27 (29:31:33:35), turn.
Slide other 28 (30:32:34:36) sts onto spare needles.
Row 2 Sl1, k27 (29:31:33:35), turn.
Working back and forth on these 28 (30:32:34:36) sts, rep these last two rows 12 (14:16:18:20) more times.

Heel shaping

Row 1 Sl1, p15 (16:17:18:19), p2tog, p1, turn.
Row 2 Sl1, k5, ssk2tog, k1, turn.
Row 3 Sl1, p6, p2tog, p1, turn.
Row 4 Sl1, k7, ssk2tog, k1, turn.
Cont in this way, taking one more stitch in each row until the row 'sl1, k13 (15:15:17:17), ssk2tog, k1, turn' has been worked. (For AS and AL, do NOT turn at end of last of these rows.)
CXL, AM, AXL only:
Next row Sl1, p14 (-:16:-:18) p2tog, turn.
Next row Sl1, k14 (-:16:-:18), ssk2tog.
All sizes: 16 (18:18:20:20) sts.

Pick up for instep

Pick up knitwise 14 (15:16:17:18) sts down side of heel flap, place marker.
Knit 28 (30:32:34:36) sts from cuff, place marker,

pick up knitwise 14 (15:16:17:18) sts up side of heel flap, k8 (9:9:10:10). 72 (78:82:88:92) sts.

Shape instep

Round 1 Knit to 3 sts before first marker, k2tog, k1 (marker), knit to next marker, k1, ssk2tog, knit to end. 70 (76:80:86:90) sts.
Round 2 Knit.
Rep these last two rounds until 58 (60:64:68:72) sts remain.

Foot

Knit 41 (45:48:51:57) rounds.**

Divide for toes

K5 (6:6:7:7), slip next 9 (9:10:10:11) sts (marker), and next 9 (9:10:10:11) sts onto waste yarn, cast on 4 sts, k rem 33 (36:38:41:43) sts.

Main toe section

Working on these 42 (46:48:52:54) sts, cont as follows:
Round 1 K4 (5:5:6:6), k2tog, k2, ssk2tog, knit to 3 sts before marker, k2tog, k1 (marker), k1, ssk2tog, knit to end. 38 (42:44:48:50) sts.
Round 2 Knit.
Round 3 K3 (4:4:5:5), k2tog, k2, ssk2tog, knit to 3 sts before marker, k2tog, k1 (marker), k1, ssk2tog, knit to end. 34 (38:40:44:46) sts.
Round 4 Knit.
Round 5 Knit to 3 sts before first marker, k2tog, k1 (marker), k1, ssk2tog, knit to end. 32 (36:38:42:44) sts.
Round 6 Knit.
Rep these last two rounds until 20 sts remain.
Knit to marker.

Rearrange sts so that the 10 sts after marker are on one needle with the 10 sts either side of beginning and end of round on another needle.
Graft toe together using Kitchener stitch (see page 10).

Big toe

Return sts on waste yarn to needles. With RS facing, knit across 9 (9:10:10:11) sts (marker), 9 (9:10:10:11) sts, pick up 4 sts from cast-on edge of Main toe section. 22 (22:24:24:26) sts.

***Round 1** K8(8:9:9:10), k2tog, k2, ssk2tog, knit to end. 20 (20:22:22:24) sts.

Round 2 Knit.

Round 3 K8 (8:9:9:10), k2tog, ssk2tog, knit to end. 18 (18:20:20:22) sts.

Rounds 4–10 Knit.

Round 11 K1, ssk2tog, knit to last 3 sts, k2tog, k1. 16 (16:18:18:20) sts.

Round 12 Knit.

Rep these last two rounds until 12 sts remain.

Rearrange sts so that the first 6 sts are on one needle with the last 6 sts on another needle.
Graft toe together using Kitchener stitch (see page 10).***

Right sock

Work as for Left sock from ** to **.

Divide for toes

Next round K33 (36:38:41:43), slip next 9 (9:10:10:11) sts (marker), and next 9 (9:10:10:11) sts onto waste yarn, cast on 4 sts, knit last 5 (6:6:7:7) sts.

Main toe section

Working on these 42 (46:48:52:54) sts, cont as follows:

Round 1 Knit to 3 sts before marker, k2tog, k1 (marker), k1, ssk2tog, k to last 10 (11:11:12:12) sts, k2tog, k2, ssk2tog, knit to end. 38 (42:44:48:50) sts.

Round 2 Knit.

Round 3 Knit to 3 sts before marker, k2tog, k1 (marker), k1, ssk2tog, k to last 9 (10:10:11:11) sts, k2tog, ssk2tog, knit to end. 34 (38:40:44:46) sts.

Round 4 Knit.

Round 5 Knit to 3 sts before first marker, k2tog, k1 (marker), k1, ssk2tog, knit to end. 32 (36:38:42:44) sts.

Round 6 Knit.

Rep these last two rounds until 20 sts remain.
Knit to marker.

Rearrange sts so that the 10 sts after marker are on one needle with the 10 sts either side of beginning and end of round on another needle.
Graft toe together using Kitchener stitch (see page 10).

Big toe

Return sts on waste yarn to needles. With RS facing, knit across 9 (9:10:10:11) sts (marker), 9 (9:10:10:11) sts, pick up 4 sts from cast-on edge of Main Toe section. 22 (22:24:24:26) sts.
Knit to marker.
Work as for Big toe of Left sock from *** to ***.

Finishing

Sew in all ends.

going **dotty**

These double-thickness socks are not only very snug and warm to wear on chilly winter days, but they are reversible, too, giving you two pairs of socks in one!

Sizes

CXL (AS:AM:AL:AXL)

(See page 7.)

Materials

1 (1:1:1:1) 3½ oz (100 g) balls of Schoeller & Stahl Fortissima Colori in main color M (dark green/Loden 1089) and 2 (2:2:2:2) balls of A (green-orange/Hummingbird 2419)

Set of US 2 (2.75 mm) double-pointed knitting needles

Gauge/Tension

36 sts and 44 rows to 4 in (10 cm) over stockinette/stocking stitch using US 2 (2.75 mm) needles

Abbreviations

cm centimeter(s); **cont** continu(e)(ing); **g** gram(s); **in** inch(es); **inc** increase; **k** knit; **mm** millimeter; **oz** ounce(s); **p** purl; **patt** pattern; **rep** repeat; **RS** right side; **sl1** slip one stitch; **ssk2tog** [slip next stitch] twice, insert left needle into front of slipped stitches and knit together; **st(s)** stitch(es); **tog** together; **tbl** through back of loops.

Pattern note

Slip all sts purlwise. After every knit st, slipped st should be worked with yarn at front (outside) of work. Before every purl st, slipped st should be worked with yarn at back (inside) of work.

Left sock

Using yarn M, cast on 96 (102:108:114:120) sts.
Divide sts between 3 needles, join and place marker.
Working in the round:
Foundation round *(RS)* *K2tog, k1, p2tog, p1, rep
from * to end. 64 (68:72:76:80) sts.

Rib

Round 1 *K2, p2, rep from * to end.
Rep this last round 14 more times.

Cuff

Increase round Inc once in every st to end.
128 (136:144:152:160) sts.
Foundation round 1 Using yarn M, *k1, sl1, rep from
* to end.
Foundation round 2 Using yarn A, *sl1, p1, rep from
* to end.
Commence patt
Round 1 Using yarn M, *k1, sl1, rep from * to end.
Round 2 Using yarn A, *sl1, p1, rep from * to end.
Rounds 3 to 6 As rounds 1 and 2, twice.
Round 7 Using yarn M, *[k1, sl1] 3 (3:4:5:5) times, [sl1,
p1] 2 (3:3:3:4) times, [k1, sl1] 9 (8:9:10:9) times, [sl1,
p1] 2 (3:3:3:4) times, [k1, sl1] 9 times, [sl1, p1] 2
(3:3:3:4) times, [k1, sl1] 5 times, rep from * once more.
Round 8 Using yarn A, *[sl1, p1] 3 (3:4:5:5) times, [k1,
sl1] 2 (3:3:3:4) times, [sl1, p1] 9 (8:9:10:9) times, [k1,
sl1] 2 (3:3:3:4) times, [sl1, p1] 9 times, [k1, sl1] 2
(3:3:3:4) times, [sl1, p1] 5 times, rep from * once more.
Round 9 Using yarn M, *[k1, sl1] 2 (2:3:4:4) times, [sl1,
p1] 4 (5:5:5:6) times, [k1, sl1] 7 (6:7:8:7) times, [sl1, p1]
4 (5:5:5:6) times, [k1, sl1] 7 times, [sl1, p1] 4 (5:5:5:6)
times, [k1, sl1] 4 times, rep from * once more.
Round 10 Using yarn A, *[sl1, p1] 2 (2:3:4:4) times, [k1,
sl1] 4 (5:5:5:6) times, [sl1, p1] 7 (6:7:8:7) times, [k1, sl1]
4 (5:5:5:6) times, [sl1, p1] 7 times, [k1, sl1] 4 (5:5:5:6)
times, [sl1, p1] 4 times, rep from * once more.

Rounds 11 and 12 As rounds 9 and 10. Round 12 as
round 10.
Round 13 Using yarn M, *[k1, sl1] 1 (1:2:3:3) times,
[sl1, p1] 6 (7:7:7:8) times, [k1, sl1] 5 (4:5:6:5) times, [sl1,
p1] 6 (7:7:7:8) times, [k1, sl1] 5 times, [sl1, p1] 6
(7:7:7:8) times, [k1, sl1] 3 times, rep from * once more.
Round 14 Using yarn A, *[sl1, p1] 1 (1:2:3:3) times, [k1,
sl1] 6 (7:7:7:8) times, [sl1, p1] 5 (4:5:6:5) times, [k1, sl1]
6 (7:7:7:8) times, [sl1, p1] 5 times, [k1, sl1] 6 (7:7:7:8)
times, [sl1, p1] 3 times, rep from * once more.
Round 15 As round 13.
Rounds 15 to 18 As rounds 13 and 14, twice.
Rounds 19 to 22 As rounds 9 and 10, twice.
Rounds 23 and 24 As rounds 7 and 8.
Rounds 25 to 30 As rounds 1 and 2, 3 times.
Round 31 Using yarn M, *[sl1, p1] 1 (1:1:1:2) times,
[k1, sl1] 9 (8:9:10:9) times, [sl1, p1] 2 (3:3:3:4) times,
[k1, sl1] 9 times, [sl1, p1] 2 (3:3:3:4) times, [k1, sl1] 8
(8:9:10:9) times, [sl1, p1] 1 (2:2:2:2) times, rep from *
once more.
Round 32 Using yarn A, *[k1, sl1] 1 (1:1:1:2) times, [sl1,
p1] 9 (8:9:10:9) times, [k1, sl1] 2 (3:3:3:4) times, [sl1, p1]
9 times, [k1, sl1] 2 (3:3:3:4) times, [sl1, p1] 8 (8:9:10:9)
times, [k1, sl1] 1 (2:2:2:2) times, rep from * once more.
Round 33 Using yarn M, *[sl1, p1] 2 (2:2:2:3) times, [k1,
sl1] 7 (6:7:8:7) times, [sl1, p1] 4 (5:5:5:6) times, [k1, sl1]
7 times, [sl1, p1] 4 (5:5:5:6) times, [k1, sl1] 6 (6:7:8:7)
times, [sl1, p1] 2 (3:3:3:3) times, rep from * once more.
Round 34 Using yarn A, *[k1, sl1] 2 (2:2:2:3) times, [sl1,
p1] 7 (6:7:8:7) times, [k1, sl1] 4 (5:5:5:6) times, [sl1, p1]
7 times, [k1, sl1] 4 (5:5:5:6) times, [sl1, p1] 6 (6:7:8:7)
times, [k1, sl1] 2 (3:3:3:3) times, rep from * once more.
Rounds 35 and 36 As rounds 33 and 34.
Round 37 Using yarn M, *[sl1, p1] 3 (3:3:3:4) times,
[k1, sl1] 5 (4:5:6:5) times, [sl1, p1] 6 (7:7:7:8) times, [k1,
sl1] 5 times, [sl1, p1] 6 (7:7:7:8) times, [k1, sl1] 4
(4:5:6:5) times, [sl1, p1] 3 (4:4:4:4) times, rep from *
once more.

Round 38 Using yarn A, *[k1, sl1] 3 (3:3:3:4) times, [sl1, p1] 5 (4:5:6:5) times, [k1, sl1] 6 (7:7:7:8) times, [sl1, p1] 5 times, [k1, sl1] 6 (7:7:7:8) times, [sl1, p1] 4 (4:5:6:5) times, [k1, sl1] 3 (4:4:4:4) times, rep from * once more.
Rounds 39 to 42 As rounds 37 and 38, twice.
Rounds 43 to 46 As rounds 33 and 34, twice.
Rounds 47 and 48 As rounds 31 and 32.
These 48 rounds form patt.
Cont in patt for 72 more rounds.

Heel flap

Using yarn M, [k1, sl1] 16 (17:18:19:20) times.
Return to start of round and using yarn A, [sl1, p1] 16 (17:18:19:20) times, turn.
Cont working in rows and keep stockinette/stocking stitch correct by working in knit or purl as necessary.
Row 1 Using yarn M, [sl1, p1] 32 (34:36:38:40) times, do not turn.
Row 2 Using yarn A, [k1,sl1] 32 (34:36:38:40) times, turn.
Slide other 64 (68:72:76:80) sts onto spare needles.

Working back and forth on these 64 (68:72:76:80) sts, keeping patt correct and only working full spot motifs, rep these last two rows 30 (32:34:36:38) more times.
Separate sts by slipping all sts in yarn M onto one needle and all sts in yarn A onto another needle. (32 (34:36:38:40) st in each color.)

Heel shaping

Working on yarn M sts with yarn M:
Row 1 Sl1, p17 (18:19:20:21), p2tog, p1, turn.
Row 2 Sl1, k5, ssk2tog, k1, turn.
Row 3 Sl1, p6, p2tog, p1, turn.
Row 4 Sl1, k7, ssk2tog, k1, turn.
Cont in this way, taking one more stitch in each row until the row 'sl1, k15 (17:17:19:19), ssk2tog, k1, turn' has been worked. For AS and AL, do NOT turn at end of this last row.
CXL, AM, AXL only:
Next row Sl1, p16 (-:18:-:20), p2tog, turn.
Next row Sl1, k16 (-:18:-:20), ssk2tog.
All sizes: 18 (20:20:22:22) sts.

Working on yarn A sts with yarn A:
Row 1 Sl1, k17 (18:19:20:21), ssk2tog, k1, turn.
Row 2 Sl1, p5, p2tog, k1, turn.
Row 3 Sl1, k6, ssk2tog, k1, turn.
Row 4 Sl1, p7, p2tog, p1, turn.
Cont in this way, taking one more stitch in each row until the row 'sl1, p15 (17:17:19:19), p2tog, k1, turn' has been worked. For AS and AL, do NOT turn at end of this last row.

CXL, AM, AXL only:
Next row Sl1, k16 (-:18:-:20), ssk2tog, turn.
Next row Sl1, p16 (-:18:-:20), p2tog.
All sizes: 18 (20:20:22:22) sts.

Pick up for instep

Using yarn M, pick up knitwise 16 (17:18:19:20) sts down side of outer heel flap, place marker.
Patt appropriate 32 (34:36:38:40) sts from cuff, place marker.
Pick up knitwise 16 (17:18:19:20) sts up side of outer heel flap, patt to end of round.
Using yarn A, pick up purlwise 16 (17:18:19:20) sts down side of inner heel flap, patt appropriate 32 (34:36:38:40) sts from cuff, pick up purlwise 16 (17:18:19:20) sts up side of outer heel flap, patt to end of round.

Rearrange the resulting 164 (176:184:196:204) sts as alternate yarn M and yarn A sts.

Shape instep

Round 1 Using yarn M, patt to 2 M sts before first marker, k2tog (marker), patt to next marker (markers), ssk2tog, patt to end.
Round 2 Using yarn A, patt to 2 A sts before first marker, p2tog (marker), patt to next marker (markers), p2togtbl, patt to end. 160 (172:180:192:200) sts.
Round 3 Using yarn M, patt to end.
Round 4 Using yarn A, patt to end.
Rep these last two rounds until 128 (136:144:152:160) sts remain.

Foot

Cont straight in patt as set until work measures 6¼ (7:7½:7¾:7¾) in/16 (18:19:20:20) cm from back of heel, ending after a yarn A round.

Separate sts by slipping all sts in yarn A onto one set of needles and all sts in yarn M onto waste yarn. (64 (68:72:76:80)sts in each set.)

Decrease for toe

Working on yarn A sts only, with yarn A:
Round 1 Purl to 3 sts before first marker, p2tog, p1 (marker), p1, p2togtbl, purl to 3 sts before next marker, p2tog, p1 (marker), p1, p2togtbl, purl to end. 60 (64:68:72:76) sts.
Round 2 Purl.
Rep these last two rounds until 24 sts remain.
Knit to first marker.

Rearrange sts so that the first 6 and last 6 sts of the round are on one needle with the 12 middle sts on another needle.
Graft toe together using Kitchener stitch (see page 10).

Return yarn M sts to needles and, working with yarn M:
Round 1 Knit to 3 sts before first marker, k2tog, k1 (marker), k1, ssk2tog, knit to 3 sts before next marker, k2tog, k1 (marker), k1, ssk2tog, knit to end. 60 (64:68:72:76) sts.
Round 2 Knit.
Rep these last two rounds until 24 sts remain.
Knit to first marker.

Rearrange sts so that the first 6 and last 6 sts of the round are on one needle with the 12 middle sts on another needle.
Graft toe together using Kitchener stitch (see page 10).

Right sock

Work as for Left sock, reversing yarns M and A if desired.

Finishing

Sew in all ends.

in **jest**

Creating a thick, felted fabric gives you the opportunity to sculpt the shape required for this pair of jester boots. Add the bells and you can entertain in your slippers!

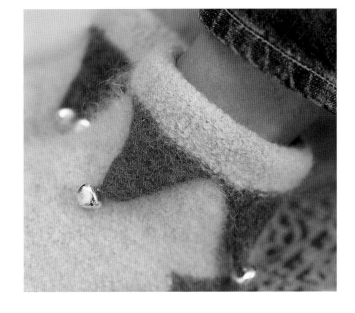

Sizes

CL–CXL (AS–AM:AM-AL)

(See page 7.)

Materials

2 (2:2) 1¾oz (50 g) balls of Rowan Kid Classic in main color M (grey/Crystal 840) and 1 (1:1) ball each in A (dark pink/Frilly 844) and B (dark green/Spruce 853)

Pair of US 8 (5 mm) knitting needles

Set of US 8 (5 mm) double-pointed knitting needles

10 small bells

Sewing needle and thread

Gauge/Tension

19 sts and 25 rows to 4 in (10 cm) over stockinette/stocking stitch using US 8 (5 mm) needles

Abbreviations

cm centimeter(s); **cont** continu(e)(ing); **g** gram(s); **in** inch(es); **inc** increase; **k** knit; **M1** make one st by picking up strand between needles and working into the back of it; **mm** millimeter; **oz** ounce(s); **p** purl; **rep** repeat; **RS** right side; **st(s)** stitch(es); **tog** together; **wrap next st** wrap next stitch by slipping next stitch from left to right needle, take yarn to opposite side of work between needles, slip stitch back onto the left needle – when working wrapped stitches, work through both the stitch and the wrap.

Triangles

(make 4 in yarn A and 4 in yarn B)

Make and leave on needles until required.

Using US 8 (5 mm) needles, cast on 2 sts.

Row 1 (RS) Inc once in both sts. 4 sts.

Row 2 Purl.

Row 3 Knit.

Row 4 Purl.

Row 5 K1, M1, knit to last st, M1, k1. *6 sts.*

Rep these last 4 rows until 12 (14:16) sts on needle.

Work 1 row.

Next row Knit to last st, M1, k1. 13 (15:17) sts.

Left sock

Using US 8 (5 mm) double-pointed needles and yarn M, *knit across 13 (15:17) sts from a Triangle in yarn A, then 13 (15:17) sts from Triangle in yarn B, rep from * once more (4 Triangles used).

Divide sts between 3 needles, join and place marker. 52 (60:68) sts.

Cuff

Working in the round:

Knit 50 (55:60) rounds.

Heel shaping

Change to yarn A.

K12 (14:16), wrap next st, turn.

Row 1 P24 (28:32), wrap next st, turn.

Slide other 26 (30:34) sts (sts between wrapped sts) onto spare needles.

Row 2 K23 (27:31), wrap next st, turn.

Row 3 P22 (26:30), wrap next st, turn.

Cont in this way, working 1 more st before wrapping next st on each row until the following row has been worked:

P12, wrap next st, turn.

Next row K12, work wrapped st, wrap next st, turn.

Next row P13, work wrapped st, wrap next st, turn.

Next row K14, work double-wrapped st by knitting through the st and the two wraps together, wrap next st, turn.

Next row P15, work double-wrapped st by purling through the st and the two wraps together, wrap next st, turn.

Cont in this way, working 1 more st on each row before wrapping next st until the following row has been worked: P23 (27:31), work double-wrapped st, wrap next st, turn.

Change to yarn M.

Next row/round K24 (28:32) work double-wrapped st, knit across 26 (30:34) sts held on spare needles, work remaining double-wrapped st, k12 (14:16).

Foot

Knit 58 (64:70) rounds.

Decrease for toe

Round 1 K1, k2tog, knit to last 3 sts, k2tog, k1. 50 (58:66) sts.

Rounds 2 and 3 Knit.

Rep the last 3 rounds until 4 sts remain.

Break yarn, thread through remaining sts and draw up tightly. Leave a long end for finishing.

Right sock

Work as for Left sock, reversing the order of triangles and working Heel shaping in yarn B.

Finishing

Using the long end left at the Toe, work a line of running stitch along the center of the top of the sock from the toe to halfway up the foot. Draw up to curl toe upwards and secure end. Sew in all ends.

Machine-wash socks: start at a low temperature and repeat on a higher setting as necessary to achieve a firm, felted fabric. Pull socks into shape while damp and allow to dry naturally. Once dry, attach a bell to each Toe and each point of Triangles.

slouch **socks**

Knitted in a luxurious silk-blend yarn, these casual socks are perfect for lazy Sunday mornings on the sofa, reading the papers. The ruched effect is knitted in, so don't try to pull them up!

Sizes

CS (CM:CL:CXL:AS:AM:AL)

(See page 7.)

Materials

2 (2:2:2:3:3:4) 1¾ oz (50 g) balls of Regia Silk 6-ply in pale blue/Pale Blue 054

Set of US 3 (3.25 mm) double-pointed needles

Gauge/Tension

24 sts and 34 rows to 4 in (10 cm) over stockinette/stocking stitch using US 3 (3.25 mm) needles

Abbreviations

cm centimeter(s); **g** gram(s); **in** inch(es); **k** knit; **mm** millimeter; **oz** ounce(s); **p** purl; **rep** repeat; **RS** right side; **sl1** slip one stitch; **ssk2tog** [slip next stitch] twice, insert left needle into front of slipped stitches and knit together; **st(s)** stitch(es); **tog** together; **tuck4/5/6/7/8** insert right needle into next st as if to knit then through back of loop of same st 4/5/6/7/8 rows below and knit two stitches together.

Socks (both alike)

Cast on 48 (54:60:66:72:78:84) sts.

Divide sts between 3 needles, join and place marker. Working in the round:

Foundation round *K2tog, k1, p2tog, p1, rep from * to end. 32 (36:40:44:48:52:56) sts.

Rib

Round 1 (RS) *K2, p2, rep from * to end.

Rep this last round 9 more times.

Cuff

Knit 8 (9:10:11:12:13:14) rounds.

**Tuck round 1 *Tuck4, tuck5, tuck6, tuck7, [tuck8] 0 (0:1:3:4:4:5) times, tuck7, tuck6, tuck5, tuck4, k3 (4:4:4:4:5:6), rep from * twice, tuck4, tuck5, tuck6, tuck7, [tuck8] 0 (0:1:3:4:4:5) times, tuck7, tuck6, tuck5, tuck4, k2 (4:5:3:4:6:5).

Knit 8 (9:10:11:12:13:14) rounds.

Tuck round 2 K2 (4:5:3:4:6:5), *tuck4, tuck5, tuck6, tuck7, [tuck8] 0 (0:1:3:4:4:5) times, tuck7, tuck6, tuck5, tuck4, k3 (4:4:4:4:5:6), rep from * twice, tuck4, tuck5, tuck6, tuck7, [tuck8] 0 (0:1:3:4:4:5) times, tuck7, tuck6, tuck5, tuck4.

Knit 7 (8:9:10:11:12:13) rounds.

Next round Knit to last 4 sts, tuck4, tuck5, tuck6, tuck7.

Tuck round 3 *[Tuck8] 0 (0:1:3:4:4:5) times, tuck7, tuck6, tuck5, tuck4, k3 (4:4:4:4:5:6), tuck4, tuck5, tuck6, tuck7, rep from * once, [tuck8] 0 (0:1:3:4:4:5) times, tuck7, tuck6, tuck5, tuck4, k6 (8:9:7:8:10:9).

Knit 8 (9:10:11:12:13:14) rounds.**

Rep from ** to ** once more, followed by tuck round 1 once more.

Heel flap

K8 (9:10:11:12:13:14), turn.

Row 1 Sl1, p15 (17:19:21:23:25:27), turn.

Slide other 16 (18:20:22:24:26:28) sts onto spare needles.

Row 2 Sl1, k15 (17:19:21:23:25:27), turn.

Working back and forth on these 16 (18:20:22:24:26:28) sts, rep these last 2 rows 7 (8:9:10:11:12:13) more times.

Heel shaping

Row 1 Sl1, p9 (10:11:12:13:14:15), p2tog, p1, turn.

Row 2 Sl1, k5, ssk2tog, k1, turn.

Row 3 Sl1, p6, p2tog, p1, turn.

Row 4 Sl1, k7, ssk2tog, k1, turn.

Rep last 2 rows 0 (1:1:2:2:3:3) times more. (For CM, CXL and AM, do NOT turn at the end of last of these rows.)

CS, CL, AS, AL only:

Next row Sl1, p8 (-:10:-:12:-:14), p2tog, turn.

Next row Sl1, k8 (-:10:-:12:-:14), ssk2tog.

All sizes: 10 (12:12:14:14:16:16) sts.

Pick up for instep

Pick up knitwise 8 (9:10:11:12:13:14) sts down side of heel flap, place marker.

Knit 16 (18:20:22:24:26:28) sts from cuff, place marker, pick up knitwise 8 (9:10:11:12:13:14) sts up side of heel flap,

k5 (6:6:7:7:8:8). 42 (48:52:58:62:68:72) sts.

Shape instep

Round 1 Knit to 3 sts before first marker, k2tog, k1 (marker), knit to next marker (marker), k1, ssk2tog, knit to end. 40 (46:50:56:60:66:70) sts.

Round 2 Knit.

Rep these last two rounds until 32 (36:40:44:48:52:56) sts remain.

Foot
Knit 20 (24:28:32:40:48:56) rounds.

Decrease for toe
Round 1 Knit to 3 sts before first marker, k2tog, k1 (marker), k1, ssk2tog, knit to 3 sts before next marker, k2tog, k1 (marker), k1, ssk2tog, knit to end.
28 (32:36:40:44:48:52) sts.
Round 2 Knit.
Rep these last two rounds until 16 sts remain.
Knit to first marker.

Rearrange sts so that the first 4 and last 4 sts of the round are on one needle with the 8 middle sts on another needle.
Graft toe together using Kitchener stitch (see page 10).

Finishing
Sew in all ends.

winter **warmers**

An attractive cable panel transforms these rugged socks from practical to delightful – your toes stay snug, toasty, and charmingly attired through the coldest days of the year.

Sizes

CXL (AS:AM:AL)

(See page 7.)

Materials

2 (2:3:3) 1¾oz (50 g) balls of Regia Silk 6-ply in dark green/Fir 71

Set of US 3 (3.25 mm) double-pointed knitting needles

Gauge/Tension

24 sts and 34 rows to 4 in (10 cm) over stockinette/stocking stitch using US 3 (3.25 mm) needles

Abbreviations

C4B slip next two stitches onto a cable needle and hold at back of work, knit next two stitches from left-hand needle then knit two stitches from cable needle; **C4F** slip next two stitches onto a cable needle and hold at front of work, knit next two stitches from left-hand needle then knit two stitches from cable needle; **cm** centimeters; **cont** continu(e)(ing); **g** gram(s); **in** inch; **k** knit; **mm** millimeter; **oz** ounce(s); **p** purl; **patt** pattern; **rep** repeat; **RS** right side; **sl1** slip one stitch; **ssk2tog** [slip next stitch] twice, insert left needle into front of slipped stitches and knit together; **st(s)** stitch(es); **T4B** slip next two stitches onto a cable needle and hold at back of work, knit next two stitches from left-hand needle then purl two stitches from cable needle; **T4F** slip next two stitches onto a cable needle and hold at front of work, purl next two stitches from left-hand needle then knit two stitches from cable needle; **tog** together.

Socks (both alike)

Cast on 48 (52:56:60) sts.
Divide sts between 3 needles, join and place marker.

Rib

Working in the round:
Round 1 (RS) [K1, p1] to end.
Rep this last round 11 more times.

Cuff

Round 13 P10 (12:14:16), work row 1 of Chart, p10 (12:14:16).
This round places Chart.
Cont as set for 47 rounds, repeating Chart as necessary.

Heel flap

Purl 10 (12:14:15), turn.
Row 1 Sl1, p19 (23:27:29), turn.
Slide other 28 (28:28:30) sts onto spare needles.
Row 2 Sl1, k19 (23:27:29), turn.
Working back and forth on these 20 (24:28:30) sts, rep these last two rows 9 (11:13:14) more times.

Heel shaping

Row 1 Sl1, p11 (13:15:16), p2tog, p1, turn.
Row 2 Sl1, k5, ssk2tog, k1, turn.
Row 3 Sl1, p6, p2tog, p1, turn.
Row 4 Sl1, k7, ssk2tog, k1, turn.
Cont in this way, taking one more stitch in each row until the row 'sl1, k9 (11:13:15), ssk2tog, k1, turn' has been worked. (For AL, do NOT turn at end of last of these rows.)
CXL, AS, AM only:
Next Row Sl1, p10 (12:14:-), p2tog, turn.
Next Row Sl1, k10 (12:14:-), ssk2tog.
All sizes: 12 (14:16:18) sts.

Pick up for instep

Pick up knitwise 10 (12:13:15) sts down side of heel flap, place marker, p0 (0:0:1), patt 28 (row 1 of Chart) from cuff, p0 (0:0:1), place marker, pick up knitwise 10 (12:13:15) sts up side of heel flap, k6 (7:8:9). 60 (66:70:78) sts.

Shape instep

Round 1 Purl to 3 sts before first marker, p2tog tbl, p1 (1:1:2), patt 28 sts, p1 (1:1:2), p2tog, purl to end.
Round 2 Patt.
Rep these last two rounds until 48 (52:56:60) sts remain.

Foot

Work 36 (40:44:48) rounds in patt as set.

Decrease for toe

CXL, AS only:
Round 1 Knit to marker (marker), k1, ssk2tog, knit to 3 sts before next marker, k2tog, k1 (marker), knit to end. 46 (50:-:-) sts.
Rep this last round until 40 (48:-:-) sts remain.
All sizes
Next round Knit.
Next round Knit to 3 sts before marker, k2tog, k1 (marker), k1, ssk2tog, knit to 3 sts before next marker, k2tog, k1 (marker), k1, ssk2tog, knit to end.
36 (44:52:56) sts.
Rep these last two rounds until 16 sts remain.
Knit to marker.

Rearrange sts so that the first 4 and last 4 sts of the round are on one needle with the 8 middle sts on another needle.
Graft toe together using Kitchener stitch (see page 10).

Finishing

Sew in all ends.

Winter warmers sock chart

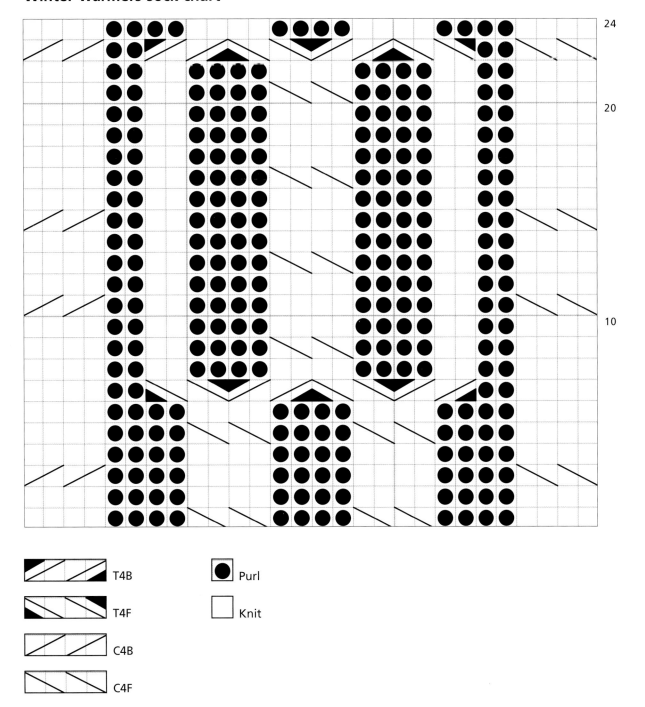

24

20

10

	T4B
	T4F
	C4B
	C4F

| ● | Purl |
| | Knit |

felted **booties**

Don't worry if these booties look huge when you are knitting them, once felted they will shrink down to a dense fabric that is very warm. An ideal choice for keeping the chill from tiny toes.

Sizes

To fit

0–3 (3–6:6–12) months

Materials

2 (2:2) ¾ oz (25 g) balls of Rowan Scottish Tweed 4-ply in main color M (blue/Skye 003) and 1(1:1) ball in A (grey/Grey Mist 001)

Set of US 3 (3.25 mm) double-pointed knitting needles

Gauge/Tension

28 sts and 36 rows to 4 in (10 cm) over stockinette/stocking stitch using US 3 (3.25 mm) needles

Abbreviations

cm centimeter(s); **cont** continu(e)(ing); **g** gram(s); **in** inch(es); **k** knit; **mm** millimeter; **oz** ounce(s); **p** purl; **rep** repeat; **sl1** slip one stitch; **ssk2tog** [slip next stitch] twice, insert left needle into front of slipped stitches and knit together; **st(s)** stitch(es); **tog** together; **WS** wrong side.

Socks (both alike)

Using yarn A, cast on 28 (36:44) sts.
Divide sts between 3 needles, join and place marker.

Cuff

Working in the round:
Round 1 Knit.
Rep this last round until work measures 6 (6¼:6½) in/15 (16:17) cm.

Heel flap

Change to yarn M.
K7 (9:11), turn.
Row 1 (WS) Sl1, p13 (17:21), turn.
Slide other 14 (18:22) sts onto spare needles.
Row 2 Sl1, k13 (17:21), turn.
Working back and forth on these 14 (18:22) sts, rep these last two rows 6 (8:10) more times.

Heel shaping

Row 1 Sl1, p8 (10:12), p2tog, p1, turn.
Row 2 Sl1, k5, ssk2tog, k1, turn.
Row 3 Sl1, p6, p2tog, p1, turn.
Row 4 Sl1, k7, ssk2tog, k1, turn.
3–6 and 6–12 months only:
Cont in this way, taking in 1 more stitch in each row until the row 'sl1, k-(9:11), ssk2tog, k1, turn' has been worked. For all sizes, do NOT turn at end of last of these rows. 10 (12:14) sts.

Pick up for instep

Pick up knitwise 7 (9:11) sts down side of heel flap, place marker.
Knit 14 (18:22) sts from cuff, place marker.
Pick up knitwise 7 (9:11) sts up side of heel flap, k5 (6:7). 38 (48:58) sts.

Shape instep

Round 1 Knit to 3 sts before first marker, k2tog, k1 (marker), knit to second marker (marker), k1, ssk2tog, knit to end. 36 (46:56) sts.
Round 2 Knit.
Rep these last two rounds until 28 (36:44) sts remain.

Foot

Knit 8 (10:14) rounds.

Decrease for toe

Round 1 Knit to 3 sts before first marker, k2tog, k1 (marker), k1, ssk2tog, knit to 3 sts before next marker, k2tog, k1 (marker), k1, ssk2tog, knit to end. 24 (32:40) sts.
Round 2 Knit.
Rep these last two rounds until 8 sts remain.
Knit to first marker.

Rearrange sts so that the first 2 and last 2 sts of the round are on one needle with the 8 middle sts on another needle.
Graft toe together using Kitchener stitch (see page 10).

Finishing

Sew in all ends.
Machine wash socks: start at a low temperature and repeat on a higher setting as necessary to achieve a firm, felted fabric. Pull socks into shape while damp and allow to dry naturally, folding top over twice to form turn-back cuff.

felted **slipper socks**

The durability and warmth of felting is ideal for keeping feet warm on winter evenings. These slippers are knitted as large socks, then felted down to a perfect fit.

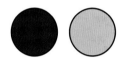

Sizes

CL–CXL (AS–AM:AM–AL)

(See page 7.)

Materials

2 (3:3) 3½ oz (100 g) balls of Rowan Big Wool in main color M (burgundy/Wild Berry 025) and 1 (1:2) 3½ oz (100 g) ball of Rowan Big Wool in A (pink/Whoosh 014)

Set of US 15 (10 mm) double-pointed knitting needles

Gauge/Tension

9½ sts and 11 rows to 4 in (10 cm) over stockinette/stocking stitch using US 15 (10 mm) needles

Abbreviations

cm centimeter(s); **g** gram(s); **in** inch(es); **k** knit; **mm** millimeter; **oz** ounce(s); **p** purl; **rep** repeat; **sl1** slip one stitch; **ssk2tog** [slip next stitch] twice, insert left needle into front of slipped stitches and knit together; **st(s)** stitch(es); **tog** together; **WS** wrong side.

Socks (both alike)

Using yarn A, cast on 28 (32:36) sts.
Divide sts between 3 needles, join and place marker.

Cuff

Working in the round:
Knit 22 (25:28) rounds.
Change to yarn M.
Knit 12 (15:18) rounds.

Heel flap

K7 (8:9), turn.
Row 1 (WS) Sl1, p13 (15:17), turn.
Slide other 14 (16:18) sts onto spare needles.
Row 2 Sl1, k13 (15:17), turn.
Working back and forth on these 14 (16:18) sts, rep these last two rows 6 (7:8) more times.

Heel shaping

Row 1 Sl1, p9 (10:11), p2tog, p1, turn.
Row 2 Sl1, k5, ssk2tog, k1, turn.
Row 3 Sl1, p6, p2tog, p1, turn.
Row 4 Sl1, k7, ssk2tog, k1, turn.
AS, AM, AL only:
Row 5 Sl1, p8, p2tog, p1, turn.
Row 6 Sl1, k9, ssk2tog, k1,turn.
AS, AM only:
Next row Sl1, p8, p2tog, turn.
Next row Sl1, k8, ssk2tog, turn.
All sizes: do NOT turn at the end of last of these rows.
10 (10:12) sts.

Pick up for instep

Pick up knitwise 7 (8:9) sts down side of heel flap, place marker, k14 (16:18) sts from cuff, place marker, pick up knitwise 7 (8:9) sts up side of heel flap, k5 (5:6).
38 (42:48) sts.

Shape instep

Round 1 Knit to 3 sts before first marker, k2tog, k1 (marker), knit to next marker (marker), k1, ssk2tog, knit to end. 36 (40:46) sts.
Round 2 Knit.
Rep these last two rounds until 28 (32:36) sts remain.

Foot

Knit 13 (16:20) rounds.

Decrease for toe

Round 1 Knit to 3 sts before first marker, k2tog, k1 (marker), k1, ssk2tog, knit to 3 sts before next marker, k2tog, k1 (marker), k1, ssk2tog, knit to end.
24 (28:32) sts.
Round 2 Knit.
Rep these last two rounds until 12 sts remain.
Knit to first marker.

Rearrange sts so that the first 3 and last 3 sts of the round are on one needle with the 6 middle sts on another needle.
Graft toe together using Kitchener stitch (see page 10).

Finishing

Sew in all ends.
Machine wash socks: start at a low temperature and repeat on a higher setting as necessary to achieve a firm, felted fabric. Pull socks into shape while damp and allow to dry naturally, folding cuff to right side to form turn-back.

well-heeled
wonders

vertical **stripes**

The garter-stitch tops give you vertical stripes, an effect not often seen on socks. Folding over the cuff reveals the more solid stripes and the fringing adds a stylish touch.

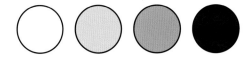

Sizes

CXL (AS:AM:AL:AXL)

(See page 7.)

Materials

1 (1:1:2:2) 3½ oz (50 g) balls of Schoeller & Stahl Fortissima in main color A (white/Brilliant White 1024) and 1 (1:1:1:1) ball each of B (pale blue/Ice 1004), C (turquoise/Turquoise 1005) and D (purple/Violet 1014).

Pair of US 2 (2.75 mm) knitting needles

Set of US 2 (2.75 mm) double-pointed knitting needles

Gauge/Tension

36 sts and 44 rows to 4 in (10 cm) over stockinette/stocking stitch using US 2 (2.75 mm) needles

Abbreviations

cm centimeter(s); **cont** continu(e)(ing); **g** gram(s); **in** inch(es); **k** knit; **mm** millimeter; **oz** ounce(s); **p** purl; **rep** repeat; **sl1** slip one stitch; **ssk2tog** [slip next stitch] twice, insert left needle into front of slipped stitches and knit together; **st(s)** stitch(es); **tog** together; **WS** wrong side.

Stripe sequence

Knit 2 rows using yarn M.
Knit 2 rows using yarn A.
Knit 2 rows using yarn B.
Knit 2 rows using yarn C.
Rep these 8 rows as necessary.
Cut yarn after each color change and leave a 6 in
(15 cm) tail of yarn at beginning and end of each stripe.
(These ends will be used to form fringes.)

Socks (both alike)

Using US 2 (2.75 mm) needles and M, cast on 72 sts.

Garter stitch top

Work 112 (120:128:136:144) rows in stripe sequence.
Cast off.
Join cast-off and cast-on edges.

Cuff

With WS facing and using US 2 (2.75 mm) double-
pointed needles and yarn M, pick up 56 (60:64:68:72)
sts around edge of cuff without yarn ends.
Divide sts between 3 needles, join and place marker.
Working in the round:
Knit 20 rounds.

Heel flap

K14 (15:16:17:18), turn.
Row 1 Sl1, p27 (29:31:33:35), turn.
Slide other 28 (30:32:34:36) sts onto spare needles.
Row 2 Sl1, k27 (29:31:33:35), turn.
Working back and forth on these 28 (30:32:34:36) sts,
rep these last two rows 12 (14:16:18:20) more times.

Heel shaping

Row 1 Sl1, p15 (16:17:18:19), p2tog, p1, turn.
Row 2 Sl1, k5, ssk2tog, k1, turn.
Row 3 Sl1, p6, p2tog, p1, turn.
Row 4 Sl1, k7, ssk2tog, k1, turn.
Cont in this way, taking one more stitch in each row until
the row 'sl1, k13 (15:15:17:17), ssk2tog, k1, turn' has
been worked. (For AS and AL, do NOT turn at end of last
of these rows.)
CXL, AM, AXL only:
Next row Sl1, p14(-:16:-:18), p2tog, turn.
Next row Sl1, k14(-:16:-:18), ssk2tog.
All sizes: 16 (18:18:20:20) sts.

Pick up for instep

Pick up knitwise 14(15:16:17:18) sts down side of heel flap,
place marker.
Knit 28 (30:32:34:36) sts from cuff, place marker.
Pick up knitwise 14 (15:16:17:18) sts up side of heel flap,
k8 (9:9:10:10). 72 (78:82:88:92) sts.

Shape instep

Round 1 Knit to 3 sts before first marker, k2tog, k1
(marker), knit to next marker (marker), k1, ssk2tog, knit to
end. 70 (76:80:86:90) sts.
Round 2 Knit.
Rep these last two rounds until 56 (60:64:68:72) sts remain.

Foot

Knit 42 (45:48:51:54) rounds.

Decrease for toe

Round 1 Knit to 3 sts before first marker, k2tog, k1
(marker), k1, ssk2tog, knit to 3 sts before next marker,
k2tog, k1 (marker), k1, ssk2tog, knit to end.
52 (56:60:64:68) sts.
Round 2 Knit.
Rep these last two rounds until 24 sts remain.
Knit to first marker.

Rearrange sts so that the first 6 and last 6 sts of the round are on one needle with the 12 middle sts on another needle.

Graft toe together using Kitchener stitch (see page 10).

Finishing

Around upper edge of garter stitch top, knot together groups of 4 yarn ends to form fringe. Trim to length desired. Sew in all remaining ends.

flower **power**

Beading is one of the easiest ways to add color and sparkle to your knitting. These pretty socks use a simple beading technique on the cuff for a stunning effect.

Sizes
CXL (AS:AM:AL)

(See page 7.)

Materials
1(1:2:2) 1¾ oz (50 g) balls of Schoeller & Stahl Fortissima in grey/Anthracite

648 (648:864:864) Rowan Beads in red/Frosted Red 1018 and 1816 (1816:2168:2168) in green/Frosted Grass Green 1022

Set of US 2 (2.75 mm) double-pointed knitting needles

Gauge/Tension
36 sts and 44 rows to 4 in (10 cm) over stockinette/stocking stitch using US 2 (2.75 mm) needles.

Abbreviations
cm centimeter(s); **cont** continu(e)(ing); **g** gram(s); **in** inch(es); **k** knit; **mm** millimeter; **oz** ounce(s); **p** purl; **rep** repeat; **RS** right side; **sl1** slip one stitch; **ssk2tog** [slip next stitch] twice, insert left needle into front of slipped stitches and knit together; **st(s)** stitch(es); **tog** together.

Pattern note
Thread beads onto the yarn in the order shown on the Charts by following row 56 of Chart A, row 56 of Chart B, row 56 of Chart A and then, for two largest sizes only, row 56 of Chart B. Continue, working across each Chart row in order.

To place a bead, slide the next bead up the yarn to wrong side of work. Knit the next stitch, allowing the bead to slip through to sit on the new stitch.

Socks (both alike)

Cast on 56 (60:64:68) sts.
Divide sts between 3 needles, join and place marker.

Cuff

Working in the round:
Round 1 (RS) [K1, p1] to end.
Rep this last round 14 more times.

Place Charts
Round 16 [Work row 1 of Chart B] 0 (0:1:1) times, k1 (2:0:1), work row 1 of Chart A, k2 (3:0:1), work row 1 of Chart B, k2 (3:0:1), work row 1 of Chart A, k1 (2:0:1).
Cont as set until all Chart rows are completed.
AM, AL only:
K7 and reposition marker to this point to indicate new start and end points of rounds.

Heel flap

K14 (15:16:17), turn.
Row 1 Sl1, p27 (29:31:33), turn.
Slide other 28 (30:32:34) sts onto spare needles.
Row 2 Sl1, k27 (29:31:33), turn.
Working back and forth on these 28 (30:32:34) sts, rep these last two rows 12 (14:16:18) more times.

Heel shaping

Row 1 Sl1, p15 (16:17:18), p2tog, p1, turn.
Row 2 Sl1, k5, ssk2tog, k1, turn.
Row 3 Sl1, p6, p2tog, p1, turn.
Row 4 Sl1, k7, ssk2tog, k1, turn.
Cont in this way, taking one more stitch in each row until the row 'sl1, k13 (15:15:17), ssktog, k1, turn' has been worked.
CXL, AM only:
Next row Sl1, p14 (-:16:-) p2tog, turn.
Next row Sl1, k14 (-:16:-), ssk2tog, turn.

All sizes: do NOT turn at end of last of these rows.
16 (18:18:20) sts.

Pick up for instep

Pick up knitwise 14 (15:16:17) sts down side of heel flap, place marker,
knit 28 (30:32:34) sts from cuff, place marker,
pick up knitwise 14 (15:16:17) sts up side of heel flap,
k8 (9:9:10). 72 (78:82:88) sts.

Shape instep

Round 1 Knit to 3 sts before first marker, k2tog, k1 (marker), knit to next marker (marker), k1, ssk2tog, knit to end. 70 (76:80:86) sts.
Round 2 Knit.
Rep these last two rounds until 56 (60:64:68) sts remain.

Foot

Knit 42 (45:48:51) rounds.

Decrease for toe

Round 1 Knit to 3 sts before first marker, k2tog, k1 (marker), k1, ssk2tog, knit to 3 sts before next marker, k2tog, k1 (marker), k1, ssk2tog, knit to end.
52 (56:60:64) sts.
Round 2 Knit.
Rep these last two rounds until 24 sts remain.
Knit to first marker.

Rearrange sts so that the first 6 and last 6 sts of the round are on one needle with the 12 middle sts on another needle.
Graft toe together using Kitchener stitch (see page 10).

Finishing

Sew in all ends.

Flower power sock chart A

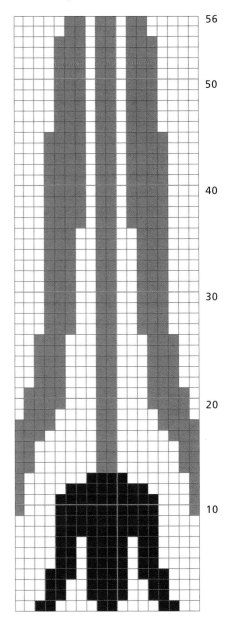

Flower power sock chart B

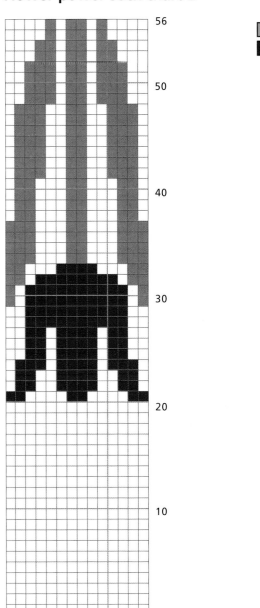

■ Place green bead
■ Place red bead

cable **cuffs**

These socks may look deceptively complex but the cable section is worked first on straight needles followed by the basic body of the sock, so they are really quite easy to knit.

Sizes
CXL (AS:AM:AL:AXL)

(See page 7.)

Materials
1 (1:1:1:1) 3½oz (100 g) balls of Schoeller & Stahl Fortissima Colori in grey-blue/Pebble 2416

Pair of US 2 (2.75 mm) knitting needles

Set of US 2 (2.75 mm) double-pointed knitting needles

Cable needle

Gauge/Tension
36 sts and 44 rows to 4 in (10 cm) over stockinette/stocking stitch using US 2 (2.75 mm) needles

Abbreviations
cm centimeter(s); **C7B** slip next four stitches onto cable needle and hold at back of work, knit next three stitches from left-hand needle then knit four stitches from cable needle; **C7F** slip next three stitches onto cable needle and hold at front of work, knit next four stitches from left-hand needle then knit three stitches from cable needle; **cont** continu(e)(ing); **g** gram(s); **in** inch(es); **k** knit; **mm** millimeter; **oz** ounce(s); **p** purl; **patt** pattern; **rep** repeat; **sl1** slip one stitch; **ssk2tog** [slip next stitch] twice, insert left needle into front of slipped stitches and knit together; **st(s)** stitch(es); **tog** together; **WS** wrong side.

Socks (both alike)

Using US 2 (2.75 mm) needles, cast on 33 sts.

Cable top

Row 1 K8, [p1, k3] 5 times, k5.
Row 2 K5, p3, [k1, p3] 5 times, k5.
Row 3 K8, p1, [C7F, p1] twice, k8.
Row 4 As row 2.
Rows 5 and 6 As rows 1 and 2.
Row 7 K5, [C7B, p1] twice, C7B, k5.
Row 8 As row 2.
Rep these last 8 rows until work measures approximately 8½ (9½:9¾:10¼:10½) in/22 (24:25:26:27) cm ending with a patt row 3 or 7.
Cast off.
Join cast-off and cast-on edges.

Cuff

With WS facing and using US 2 (2.75 mm) double-pointed needles, starting and ending at seam of cable top, pick up 56 (60:64:68:72) sts around one side edge of cable cuff.
Divide sts between 3 needles, join and place marker.
Working in the round:
Knit 2 rounds.
Round 3 [K1, p1] to end.
Rep this last round 11 more times.
Knit 56 (60:64:68:72) rounds.

Heel flap

K14 (15:16:17:18), turn.
Row 1 Sl1, p27 (29:31:33:35), turn.
Slide other 28 (30:32:34:36) sts onto spare needles.
Row 2 Sl1, k27 (29:31:33:35), turn.
Working back and forth on these 28 (30:32:34:36) sts, rep these last two rows 12 (14:16:18:20) more times.

Heel shaping

Row 1 Sl1, p15 (16:17:18:19), p2tog, p1, turn.
Row 2 Sl1, k5, ssk2tog, k1, turn.
Row 3 Sl1, p6, p2tog, p1, turn.
Row 4 Sl1, k7, ssk2tog, k1, turn.
Cont in this way, taking one more stitch in each row until the row 'sl1, k13 (15:15:17:17), ssk2tog, k1, turn' has been worked. (For AS and AL, do NOT turn at end of last of these rows.)
CXL, AM, AXL only:
Next row Sl1, p14 (-:16:-:18) p2tog, turn.
Next row Sl1, k14 (-:16:-:18), ssk2tog.
All sizes: 16 (18:18:20:20) sts.

Pick up for instep

Pick up knitwise 14 (15:16:17:18) sts down side of heel flap, place marker,
knit 28 (30:32:34:36) sts from cuff, place marker,
pick up knitwise 14 (15:16:17:18) sts up side of heel flap,
k8 (9:9:10:10). 72 (78:82:88:92) sts.

Shape instep

Round 1 Knit to 3 sts before first marker, k2tog, k1 (marker), knit to next marker (marker), k1, ssk2tog, knit to end. 70 (76:80:86:90) sts.
Round 2 Knit.
Rep these last two rounds until 56 (60:64:68:72) sts remain.

Foot

Knit 42 (45:48:51:54) rounds.

Decrease for toe

Round 1 Knit to 3 sts before first marker, k2tog, k1 (marker), k1, ssk2tog, knit to 3 sts before next marker, k2tog, k1 (marker), k1, ssk2tog, knit to end.
52 (56:60:64:68) sts.

Round 2 Knit.
Rep these last two rounds until 24 sts remain.
Knit to first marker.

Rearrange sts so that the first 6 and last 6 sts of the round are on one needle with the 12 middle sts on another needle.
Graft toe together using Kitchener stich (see page 10).

Finishing
Sew in all ends.

do the **twist**

A spiral rib pattern allows you to knit socks that mold to the shape of your foot without working a heel. A tube sock also means you get even wear, so your socks will last that much longer.

Sizes

CL–CXL (AS–AM:AM-AL)

(See page 7.)

Materials

2 (2:2) 3¾ oz (110 g) balls of Colinette Jitterbug in pink/Magenta 94

Set of US 2 (2.75 mm) double-pointed knitting needles

Cable needle

Gauge/Tension

36 sts and 44 rows to 4 in (10 cm) over stockinette/stocking stitch using US 2 (2.75 mm) needles

Abbreviations

cm centimeter(s); **cont** continu(e)(ing); **g** gram(s); **in** inch(es); **k** knit; **mm** millimeter; **oz** ounce(s); **p** purl; **rep** repeat; **RS** right side; **ssk2tog** [slip next stitch] twice, insert left needle into front of slipped stitches and knit together; **st(s)** stitch(es); **tog** together; **Tw4L** slip next three stitches onto a cable needle and hold at front of work, purl one stitch from left-hand needle then knit the three stitches from cable needle; **Tw4R** slip next stitch onto a cable needle and hold at back of work, knit three stitches from left-hand needle then purl the stitch from cable needle.

Spiral patt A
Round 1 *P2, Tw4L, rep from * 15 (17:19) times more. Rep this round throughout.

Spiral patt A uses one more st for every round than there are on needles so that the end of round moves by one st to created the spiral effect.

Spiral patt B
Round 1 *Tw4R, p2, rep from * 15 (17:19) times more. Rep this round throughout.

Spiral patt B uses one less st for every round than are on needles so that the end of round moves by one st to create the spiral effect.

Left sock
Cast on 95 (107:119) sts.
Divide sts between 3 needles, join and place marker.
Working in the round:
Round 1 Purl.
Round 2 Knit.
Rep these last two rounds once more.

Commence spiral patt A
Work in spiral patt A until work measures approximately 11¾ (13¼:15) in/30 (34:38) cm, ending after a Tw4L.

Shape toe
Round 1 [P2tog, Tw4L, p2, Tw4L] 8 (9:10) times. 87 (98:109) sts.
Round 2 [P1, Tw4L, p2, Tw4L] 8 (9:10) times.
Round 3 [P1, Tw4L, p2tog, Tw4L] 8 (9:10) times. 79 (89:99) sts.
Round 4 [P1, Tw4L] 16 (18:20) times.
Round 5 [P1, k3, p2tog, Tw4L] 8 (9:10) times. 71 (80:89) sts.
Round 6 [K3, p2, Tw4L] 7 (8:9) times, k3, p2, k3.
From this point on, beginning and end of rounds are no longer spiralling and now remain in same position.
Round 7 [K3, p2tog, p1, k3] 7 (8:9) times, k3, p2, k3.

64 (72:80) sts.
Round 8 [Tw4L, p1, k3] 8 (9:10) times.
Round 9 [P1, k1, ssk2tog, p1, k3] 8 (9:10) times. 56 (63:70) sts.
Round 10 [P1, k2, p1, k3] 8 (9:10) times.
Round 11 [P1, k2, p1, k1, ssk2tog] 8 (9:10) times. 48 (54:60) sts.
Round 12 [P1, k2] 16 (18:20) times.
Round 13 [K1, ssk2tog, k3] 8 (9:10) times. 40 (45:50) sts.
Round 14 K0 (1:0), [ssk2tog] 20 (22:25) times. 20 (23:25) sts.
Round 15 K0 (1:1), [ssk2tog] 10 (11:12) times. 10 (12:13) sts.
Break yarn, thread through sts, draw up tightly and secure on inside of sock.

Right sock
Cast on 97 (109:121) sts.
Divide sts between 3 needles, join and place marker.
Round 1 Purl.
Round 2 Knit.
Rep these last two rounds once more.

Commence spiral patt B
Work in spiral patt B until work measures 11¾ (13¼:15) in/30 (34:38) cm, ending after the first Tw4R of a round.

Shape toe
Round 1 [P2tog, Tw4R, p2, Tw4R] 8 (9:10) times. 89 (100:111) sts.
Round 2 [P1, Tw4R, p2, Tw4R] 8 (9:10) times.
Round 3 [P1, Tw4R, p2tog, Tw4R] 8 (9:10) times. 81 (91:101) sts.
Round 4 [P1, Tw4R] 16 (18:20) times.
Round 5 [P1, Tw4R, p2tog, k3] 8 (9:10) times. 73 (82:91) sts.
Round 6 P2tog, k3, p1, Tw4R, [p1, k3, p1, Tw4R] 7 (8:9) times 72 (81:90) sts.
Round 7 P1, k3, [p1, k3, p2tog, k3] 7 (8:9) times, p1, k3, p2tog. 64 (72:80) sts.

From this point on, beginning and end of rounds are no longer spiraling and now remain in the same position.

Round 8 [K3, p1] 8 (9:10) times.

Round 9 [K1, k2tog, p1, k3, p1] 16 (18:20) times. 58 (63:70) sts.

Round 10 [K2, p1, k3, p1] 8 (9:10) times.

Round 11 [K2, p1, k1, k2tog, p1] 8 (9:10) times. 50 (54:60) sts.

Round 12 [K2, p1] 16 (18:20) times.

Round 13 [K2tog, k4] 8 (9:10) times. 42 (45:50) sts.

Round 14 K0(1:0), [k2tog] to end. 21 (23:25) sts.

Round 15 K1, [k2tog] to end. 11 (12:13) sts.

Break yarn, thread through sts, draw up tightly and secure on inside of sock.

Finishing

Sew in all ends.

footlets

Sometimes you don't want the whole sock package. These short, footlet socks are perfect for wearing with sneakers. The addition of a little pompom stops them from sliding down inside your shoes.

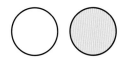

Sizes
CXL (AS:AM:AL)
(See page 7.)

Materials
1 (1:1:2:) 1¾ oz (50 g) balls of Schoeller & Stahl Fortissima in main color M (white/Brilliant White 1024) and 1 (1:1:1) ball in A (pale pink/Rose 1093)
Set of US 2 (2.75 mm) double-pointed knitting needles

Gauge/Tension
36 sts and 44 rows to 4 in (10 cm) over stockinette/stocking stitch using US 2 (2.75 mm) needles

Abbreviations
cm centimeter(s); **cont** continu(e)(ing); **g** gram(s); **in** inch(es); **k** knit; **mm** millimeter; **oz** ounce(s); **p** purl; **rep** repeat; **RS** right side; **sl1** slip one stitch; **ssk2tog** [slip next stitch] twice, insert left needle into front of slipped stitches and knit together; **st(s)** stitch(es); **tog** together.

Socks (both alike)

Using yarn A, cast on 56 (60:64:68) sts.
Divide sts between 3 needles, join and place marker.
Working in the round:
Round 1 (RS) [K1, p1] to end.
Rep this last round 5 more times.
Change to yarn M.
Knit 1 round.

Heel flap

K14 (15:16:17), turn.
Row 1 Sl1, p27 (29:31:33), turn.
Slide other 28 (30:32:34) sts onto spare needles.
Row 2 Sl1, k27 (29:31:33), turn.
Working back and forth on these 28 (30:32:34) sts, rep these last two rows 12 (14:16:18) more times.

Heel shaping

Row 1 Sl1, p15 (16:17:18), p2tog, p1, turn.
Row 2 Sl1, k5, ssk2tog, k1, turn.
Row 3 Sl1, p6, p2tog, p1, turn.
Row 4 Sl1, k7, ssk2tog, k1, turn.
Cont in this way, taking one more stitch in each row until the row 'sl1, k13 (15:15:17), ssktog, k1, turn' has been worked. (For AS and AL, do NOT turn at end of last of these rows.)
CXL, AM only:
Next row Sl1, p14 (-:16:-), p2tog, turn.
Next row Sl1, k14 (-:16:-), ssk2tog.
All sizes: 16 (18:18:20) sts.

Pick up for instep

Pick up knitwise 14 (15:16:17) sts down side of heel flap, place marker.
Knit 28 (30:32:34) sts from cuff, place marker.
Pick up knitwise 14 (15:16:17) sts up side of heel flap, k8 (9:9:10). 72 (78:82:88) sts.

Shape instep

Round 1 Knit to 3 sts before first marker, k2tog, k1 (marker), knit to next marker (marker), k1, ssk2tog, knit to end. 70 (76:80:86) sts.
Round 2 Knit.
Rep these last two rounds until 56 (60:64:68) sts remain.

Foot

Knit 42 (45:48:51) rounds.

Decrease for toe

Change to yarn A.
Round 1 Knit to 3 sts before first marker, k2tog, k1 (marker), k1, ssk2tog, knit to 3 sts before next marker, k2tog, k1 (marker), k1, ssk2tog, knit to end.
52 (56:60:64) sts.
Round 2 Knit.
Rep these last two rounds until 24 sts remain.
Knit to first marker.

Rearrange sts so that the first 6 and last 6 sts of the round are on one needle with the 12 middle sts on another needle.
Graft toe together using Kitchener stitch (see page 10).

Finishing

Sew in all ends.
Make 2 pompoms, approximately 1 in (3 cm) diameter, using A. Using photograph as a guide, attach to back of socks.

Fair Isle **stripes**

These socks have very modern-looking Fair Isle bands at intervals. They can be worked in bold colors, as here, or muted tones for a more discreet pair of socks.

Sizes

CXL (AS:AM:AL:AXL)

(See page 7.)

Materials

1 (1:1:2:2) 3½ oz (50 g) balls of Schoeller & Stahl Fortissima in main color M (Purple/Violet 1014) and 1 (1:1:1:1) ball each in A (turquoise/Turquoise 1005), B (orange/Mango 1008), C (white/Brilliant White 1024) and D (black/Black 1002)

Set of US 2 (2.75 mm) double-pointed knitting needles

Gauge/Tension

36 sts and 44 rows to 4 in (10 cm) over stockinette/stocking stitch using US 2 (2.75 mm) needles

Abbreviations

cm centimeter(s); **cont** continu(e)(ing); **g** gram(s); **in** inch(es); **k** knit; **mm** millimeter; **oz** ounce(s); **p** purl; **patt** pattern; **rep** repeat; **sl1** slip one stitch; **ssk2tog** [slip next stitch] twice, insert left needle into front of slipped stitches and knit together; **st(s)** stitch(es); **tog** together; **yrn** yarn round needle.

Patt band
Round 1 Using yarn A.
Round 2 Using yarn B.
Round 3 *2 sts using yarn C, 2 sts using yarn D, rep from * to end.
Round 4 As round 3.
Round 5 *2 sts using yarn D, 2 sts using yarn C, rep from * to end.
Round 6 As round 5.
Rounds 7 and 8 As rounds 3 and 4.
Round 9 As round 2.
Round 10 As round 1.

Left sock
Using yarn M, cast on 56 (60:64:68:72) sts.
Divide sts between 3 needles, join and place marker.

Cuff facing
Working in the round:
Purl 10 rounds.
Round 11 *P2tog, yrn, rep from * to end.
Round 12 Purl.

Cuff turndown
Work patt band (purl throughout).
Break off all contrast yarns.
Using yarn M, purl 2 rounds.

Rib
Round 24 *K1, p1, rep from * to end.
Rep this last round 11 more times.**
Knit 46 (50:54:58:62) rounds.
Work patt band (knit throughout).
Break off all contrast yarns.
Cont using yarn M only.

Heel flap
***K14 (15:16:17:18), turn.

Row 1 Sl1, p27 (29:31:33:35), turn.
Slide other 28 (30:32:34:36) sts onto spare needles.
Row 2 Sl1, k27 (29:31:33:35), turn.
Working back and forth on these 28 (30:32:34:36) sts, rep these last two rows 12 (14:16:18:20) more times.

Heel shaping
Row 1 Sl1, p15 (16:17:18:19), p2tog, p1, turn.
Row 2 Sl1, k5, ssk2tog, k1, turn.
Row 3 Sl1, p6, p2tog, p1, turn.
Row 4 Sl1, k7, ssk2tog, k1, turn.
Cont in this way, taking one more stitch in each row until the row 'sl1, k13 (15:15:17:17), ssk2tog, k1, turn' has been worked. (For AS and AL, do NOT turn at end of this last round.)
CXL, AM, AXL only:
Next row Sl1, p14 (-:16:-:18) p2tog, turn.
Next row Sl1, k14 (-:16:-:18), ssk2tog.
All sizes: 16 (18:18:20:20) sts.

Pick up for instep
Pick up knitwise 14 (15:16:17:18) sts down side of heel flap, place marker.
Knit 28 (30:32:34:36) sts from cuff, place marker.
Pick up knitwise 14 (15:16:17:18) sts up side of heel flap, k8 (9:9:10:10). 72 (78:82:88:92) sts.

Shape instep
Round 1 Knit to 3 sts before first marker, k2tog, k1 (marker), knit to next marker (marker), k1, ssk2tog, knit to end. *70(76:80:86:90) sts.*
Round 2 Knit.
Rep these last two rounds until 56(60:64:68:72) sts remain.***

Foot
Knit 31 (34:37:40:43) rounds.
Work patt band (knit throughout).

Break off all contrast yarns.
Cont using yarn M only.
Knit 1 round.

Decrease for toe
**** Round 1 Knit to 3 sts before first marker, k2tog,
k1 (marker), k1, ssk2tog, knit to 3 sts before next
marker, k2tog, k1 (marker), k1, ssk2tog, knit to end.
Round 2 Knit.
Rep these last two rounds until 24 sts remain.
Knit to first marker.

Rearrange sts so that the first 6 and last 6 sts of the
round are on one needle with the 12 middle sts on
another needle.
Graft toe together using Kitchener stitch (see page
10).****

Right sock
Work as for Left sock to **

Knit 23 (25:27:29:31) rounds.
Work patt band (knit throughout).
Knit 23 (25:27:29:31) rounds.

Work as for Left sock from *** to ***.

Foot
Work patt band (knit throughout).
Break off all contrast yarns.
Cont using yarn M only.
Knit 32 (35:38:41:44) rounds.
Work as for Left sock from **** to **** to complete.

Finishing
Sew in all ends.
Fold facing at first picot line and slip stitch cast-on edge
to back of turndown.

lovely **lace**

A lace pattern adds a touch of style and a great finish to your socks. This pattern has four repeats and you may find it easier to work with a set of five needles, one for each repeat and one to work with.

Size
AS
(See page 7.)

Materials
1 3½ oz (100 g) ball of Schoeller & Stahl Fortissima Socka Cotton Color in blue mix/Lagoon 6513
Set of US 2 (2.75 mm) double-pointed knitting needles

Gauge/Tension
32 sts and 44 rows to 4 in (10 cm) over stockinette/stocking stitch using US 2 (2.75 mm) needles

Abbreviations
cm centimeter(s); **cont** continu(e)(ing); **g** gram(s); **in** inch(es); **k** knit; **mm** millimeter; **oz** ounce(s); **psso** pass slipped stitch over; **p2sso** pass two slipped stitches over; **p** purl; **patt** pattern; **rep** repeat; **RS** right side; **sl1** slip one stitch; **sl2** slip two stitches; **ssk2tog** [slip next stitch] twice, insert left needle into front of slipped stitches and knit together; **st(s)** stitch(es); **tog** together; **wrap next st** wrap next stitch by slipping next stitch from left to right needle, take yarn to opposite side of work between needles, slip stitch back onto the left needle – when working wrapped stitches, work through both the stitch and the wrap; **yf** yarn forward.

Lace patt

Rounds 1–3 Knit.

Round 4 Sl1, *[k2tog] twice, yf, [k1, yf] 5 times, [sl1, k1, psso] twice, sl2, k1, p2sso, rep from * to last 15 sts, [k2tog] twice, yf, [k1, yf] 5 times, [sl1, k1, psso] twice, sl2, K first st from next round, p2sso (move marker to before this st).

Rep these last 4 rounds 3 more times.

Rounds 17–19 Knit.

Round 20 yf, [k1, yf] twice, *[sl1, k1, psso] twice, sl2, k1, p2sso, [k2tog] twice, yf, [k1, yf] 5 times, rep from * to last 14 sts, [sl1, k1, psso] twice, sl2, k1, p2sso, [k2tog] twice, [yf, k1] 3 times.

Rep these last 4 rounds 3 more times.

Last 32 rounds form patt.

Socks (both alike)

Cast on 64 sts.

Divide sts between 3 needles, join and place marker.

Cuff

Working in the round:

Round 1 (RS) Knit.

Round 2 Purl.

Rep these last two rounds once more.

Commence patt and cont until work measures 8 in (20 cm).

Heel shaping

K15, wrap next st, turn.

Row 1 P30, wrap next st, turn.

Slide other 32 sts (sts between wrapped sts) onto spare needles.

Row 2 K29, wrap next st, turn.

Row 3 P28, wrap next st, turn.

Cont in this way, working 1 more st on each row before wrapping next st until the following row has been worked:

p12, wrap next st, turn.

Next row K12, work wrapped st, wrap next st, turn.

Next row P13, work wrapped st, wrap next st, turn.

Next row K14, work double-wrapped st by knitting through the st and the two wraps together, wrap next st, turn.

Next row P15, work double-wrapped st by purling through the st and the two wraps together, wrap next st, turn.

Cont in this way, working 1 more st before wrapping next st on each row until the following row has been worked:

p29, work double-wrapped st, wrap next st, turn.

Next row/round K30, work double-wrapped st, place marker, patt across 32 sts held on spare needles, place marker, work remaining double-wrapped st, k15. 64 sts.

Foot

With patt panel as set on top of foot and stole sts in stockinette stitch, cont straight until work measures 7 in (18 cm) from back of heel.

Decrease for toe

Working in stockinette stitch:

Round 1 Knit to 3 sts before first marker, k2tog, k1 (marker), k1, ssk2tog, knit to 3 sts before next marker, k2tog, k1 (marker), k1, ssk2tog, knit to end.

Round 2 Knit.

Rep these last two rounds until 24 sts remain.

Knit to first marker.

Rearrange sts so that the first 6 and last 6 sts of the round are on one needle with the 12 middle sts on another needle.

Graft toe together using Kitchener stitch (see page 10).

Finishing

Sew in all ends.

classic **Fair Isle**

The festive Fair Isle design on these socks is not only attractively playful, it also increases the wearer's comfort with extra yarn inside to cushion and warm your feet.

Sizes

CXL (AS:AM:AL:AXL)

(See page 7.)

Materials

2 (2:2:2:2) 1¾ oz (50 g) balls of Schoeller & Stahl Fortissima in main color M (black/Black 1002) and 1 (1:1:1:1) ball each in A (grey/Flannel 1058), B (pale grey/Light Grey 1056) and C (cream/Natural 1048)

Set of US 2 (2.75 mm) double-pointed knitting needles

Gauge/Tension

36 sts and 44 rows to 4 in (10 cm) over stockinette/stocking stitch using US 2 (2.75 mm) needles

Abbreviations

cm centimeter(s); **cont** continu(e)(ing); **g** gram(s); **in** inch(es); **k** knit; **mm** millimeter; **oz** ounce(s); **p** purl; **rep** repeat; **RS** right side; **sl1** slip one stitch; **ssk2tog** [slip next stitch] twice, insert left needle into front of slipped stitches and knit together; **st(s)** stitch(es); **tog** together; **WS** wrong side.

Socks (both alike)

Using yarn A, cast on 68 (72:76:80:84) sts.
Divide sts between 3 needles, join and place marker.

Cuff

Working in the round:
Knit 6 rounds.
Round 7 (RS) *K1 using yarn A, p1 using yarn B, rep from * to end.
Rep this last round 14 more times.
Round 22 [Work row 1 of Chart] 17 (18:19:20:21) times.
Cont in patt from Chart as set, rep Chart as necessary.
Patt 72 (76:76:80:80) rounds more.

Heel flap

Patt 17 (18:19:20:21), turn.
Row 1 (RS) Using yarn A, [sl1, p1] 17 (18:19:20:21) times.
Slide other 34 (36:38:40:42) sts onto spare needles.
Row 2 Using yarn A, [k1, sl1] 17 (18:19:20:21) times.
Row 3 Using yarn B, [p1, sl1] 17 (18:19:20:21) times.
Row 4 Using yarn B, [sl1, k1] 17 (18:19:20:21) times.
Rep these last 4 rows 14 (14:16:16:18) more times.

Heel shaping

Using yarn A
Row 1 (WS) Sl1, p18 (19:20:21:22), p2tog, p1, turn.
Row 2 Sl1, k5, ssk2tog, k1, turn.
Row 3 Sl1, p6, p2tog, p1, turn.
Row 4 Sl1, k7, ssk2tog, k1, turn.
Cont in this way, taking one more stitch in each row until the row 'sl1, k17 (17:19:19:21), ssk2tog, k1, turn' has been worked. (For CXL, AM and AXL, do NOT turn at end of last of these rounds.)
AS, AL only:
Next row Sl1, p- (18:-:20:-), p2tog, turn.
Next row Sl1, k- (18:-:20:-), ssk2tog.
All sizes: 20 (20:22:22:24) sts.

Pick up for instep

Pick up knitwise 17 (18:19:20:21) sts down side of heel flap, place marker.
Knit across 34 (36:38:40:42) sts from cuff, place marker, pick up knitwise 17 (18:19:20:21) sts up side of heel flap, k10 (10:11:11:12). 88 (92:98:102:108) sts.

Shape instep

Round 1 Patt to 3 sts before first marker, k2tog, k1 (marker), patt to next marker (marker), k1, ssk2tog, patt to end.
Round 2 Patt.
Rep these last two rounds until 68 (72:76:80:84) sts remain.

Foot

Patt 50 (52:54:56:60) rounds.

Decrease for toe

Round 1 Using yarn A, *sl1, k1, rep from * to end.
Round 2 As round 1.
Round 3 Using yarn B, *k1, sl1, rep from * to end.
Round 4 As round 3.
These 4 rounds set toe patt.
Keeping patt correct, cont as follows:
Round 1 Patt to 3 sts before first marker, k2tog, k1 (marker), k1, ssk2tog, pattt to 3 sts before next marker, k2tog, k1 (marker), k1, ssk2tog, patt to end.
64 (68:72:76:80) sts.
Rounds 2–4 Patt.
Rep these last four rounds until 24 sts remain.
Patt to first marker.

Rearrange sts so that the first 6 and last 6 sts of the round are on one needle with the 12 middle sts on another needle.
Graft toe together using Kitchener stitch (see page 10).

Finishing

Sew in all ends.

Classic Fair Isle socks chart

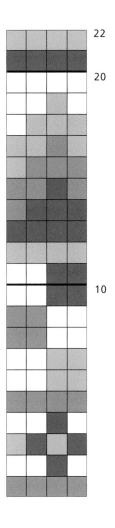

C

B

A

M

mix-&-match socks

Here are four socks that use different yarns and combine various elements from this section of the book. Each sock is unique (well, except for the matching one that makes the pair), and given here are the elements used in making them.

Common heel with a wedge toe
- Sock yarn Schoeller & Stahl Fortissima
- 1 x 1 Rib (knitted in cream)
- Stockinette/stocking stitch Cuff (knitted in dark grey)
- Common Heel (knitted in pale grey) with Instep Shaping (burgundy)
- Stockinette/stocking stitch Foot (knitted in dark grey)
- Wedge Toe (knitted in black)

Add a little rib...
- Self-patterning sock yarn Schoeller & Stahl Fortissima Colori Vine/Black 9042
- 1 x 1 Rib
- 2 x 2 rib Cuff
- Common Heel
- 2 x 2 Rib continued down top of Foot
- Wedge Toe

Short row heel and toe

- Sock yarn Regia 4-ply
- 1 x 1 Rib (knitted in pale blue)
- Stockinette/stocking stitch Cuff (knitted in navy)
- Short Row Heel (knitted in cream)
- Stockinette/stocking stitch Foot (knitted in navy)
- Short Row Toe (cream)

Vary the stitch pattern a little…

- Self-patterning sock yarn Regia Mini Ringels Jazz 5209
- 1 x 1 Rib
- Corrugated pattern cuff
- Short Row Heel
- Stockinette/stocking stitch Foot
- Short Row Toe

your own designs

Now it's your turn to indulge your creativity and design your very own pair of socks. Here are a selection of different ways of knitting each element of a sock. These have been specially designed to mix-and-match so that you can choose your favorite from each section and combine them in your design. Pick a sock weight or 4-ply yarn and a stitch pattern of your choice and get started!

Sizes
CS (CM:CL:CXL:AS:AM:AL:AXL)
(See page 7.)

Materials
The amount of yarn you require will vary depending on your choice of stitch pattern and yarn as well as size of socks. As a guide, you will need 1 (1:2:2:2:2:3:3) 1¾ oz (50 g) balls of sock weight or 4-ply yarn, with approximately 218 yd (200 m) to a 1¾ oz (50 g) ball.
Set of US 2 (2.75 mm) double-pointed knitting needles

Gauge/Tension
36 sts and 44 rows to 4 in (10 cm) over stockinette/stocking stitch using US 2 (2.75 mm) needles

Abbreviations
cm centimeter(s) **cont** continu(e)(ing); **g** gram(s); **in** inch(es) **k** knit; **mm** millimeter; **oz** ounce(s); **p** purl; **rep** repeat; **sl1** slip one stitch; **ssk2tog** [slip next stitch] twice, insert left needle into front of slipped stitches and knit together; **st(s)** stitch(es); **tog** together; **wrap next st** wrap next stitch by slipping next stitch from left to right needle, take yarn to opposite side of work between needles, slip stitch back onto the left needle – when working wrapped stitches, work through both the stitch and the wrap.

Casting on
Though it is fine to use the cable or thumb cast-on methods (see Sock-knitting basics, pages 8–15), for a cast-on edge with more give you can use one of these stretchy cast-on methods.

Stretchy cast on
Cast on 66 (72:78:84:90:96:102:108) sts.
Divide sts between double-pointed needles, join and place marker.
Round 1 *K2tog, p1, rep from * to end.
44 (48:52:56:60:64:68:72) sts.

Extra-stretchy cast on
Cast on 88 (96:104:112:120:128:136:144) sts.
Divide sts between double-pointed needles, join and place marker.
Round 1 *K2tog, p2tog, rep from * to end.
44 (48:52:56:60:64:68:72) sts.

Rib

You can adjust the rib section of your sock to suit you. For a looser fit, work the rib on a needle one size larger than that used for the rest of the sock. For a snug fit you can run thin elastic through the inside of the rib. There are also stretch sock yarns on the market that hold their shape well. The two classic rib patterns are 1 x 1 (single) rib and 2 x 2 (double) rib.

1 x 1 Rib

Round 1 *K1, p1, rep from * to end.
Rep this round 10 (10:12:12:14:14:16:16) more times.

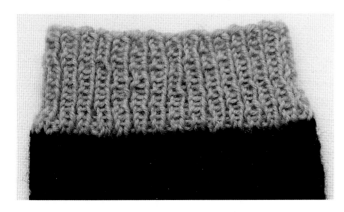

2 x 2 Rib

Round 1 *K2, p2, rep from * to end.
Rep this round 10 (10:12:12:14:14:16:16) more times.

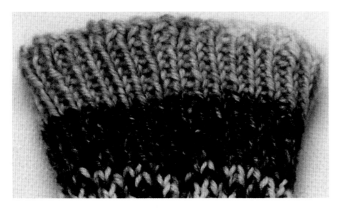

Cuff

You can let your imagination run wild here, any stitch pattern with a 4-stitch repeat will fit perfectly. Or, if you are using a self-patterning yarn, try knitting every stitch EXCEPT when the stitch to be knitted and the working yarn are the same contrast color; purl these stitches.

If you want to continue a pattern from the Cuff right down the Foot, you might want to consider centering it by starting mid-way through the repeat and completing it at the end of the round.

However you choose to knit the Cuff, work until it measures approximately 4¼ (5½:6:6¼:6¾:7:7½:7¾) in/11 (14:15:16:17:18:19:20) cm. This measurement is only a guide, you can adjust the Cuff length to suit the stitch pattern, the sock wearer, or both!

▼ Cuff detail using purl stitch

Heel

Essentially you are just knitting a corner into your tube; heels are nothing to be frightened of, just take them step-by-step like any knitting pattern. The two most often used heels are the Common Heel and the Short Row Heel.

Common heel

This is a simple heel which is worked in rows to create a 'flap' with slipped stitches at the beginning of each row. Then you pick up stitches into the convenient 'v's created by the slipped stitches along the sides of the flap and gradually decrease stitches ready to knit the Foot. This gives you a little extra room around the ankle.

▼ Common heel

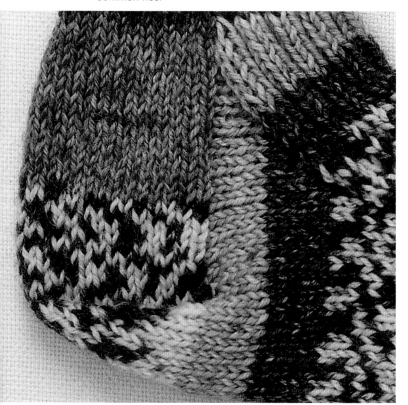

Heel flap

K11 (12:13:14:15:16:17:18), turn.
Row 1 Sl1, p21 (23:25:27:29:31:33:35), turn.
Slide other 22 (24:26:28:30:32:34:36) sts onto spare needles.
Row 2 Sl1, k21 (23:25:27:29:31:33:35), turn.
Working back and forth on these 22 (24:26:28:30:32:34:36) sts, rep these last two rows 10 (11:12:13:14:15:16:17) more times.

Heel shaping

Row 1 Sl1, p12 (13:14:15:16:17:18:19), p2tog, p1, turn.
Row 2 Sl1, k5, ssk2tog, k1, turn.
Row 3 Sl1, p6, p2tog, p1, turn.
Row 4 Sl1, k7, ssk2tog, k1, turn.
Cont in this way, taking in 1 more st each row until all the heel flap sts have been included, ending with a RS row – do NOT turn at end of this last row.
14 (14:16:16:18:18:20:20) sts.

Pick up for instep

Pick up knitwise 11 (12:13:14:15:16:17:18) sts down side of heel flap, place marker.
Knit 22 (24:26:28:30:32:34:36) sts from cuff, place marker.
Pick up knitwise 11 (12:13:14:15:16:17:18) sts up side of heel flap,
k7 (7:8:8:9:9:10:10). 58 (62:68:72:78:82:88:92) sts.

Shape instep

Round 1 Knit to 3 sts before first marker, k2tog, k1 (marker), knit to next marker (marker), k1, ssk2tog, knit to end.
Round 2 Knit.
Rep these two rounds until 44 (48:52:56:60:64:68:72) sts remain.

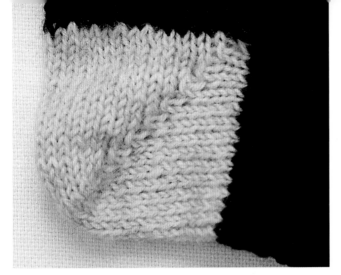

▲ Short row heel

▲ Foot

Short row heel

This is really just a mitered corner. Half the Cuff stitches are used to knit the Heel and then the same number are reunited with the Cuff to knit the Foot. This makes it very easy to continue a pattern from Cuff to Foot. As a Short Row Heel is symmetrical, it looks great knitted in a contrast color and it doesn't disrupt the flow of a self-patterning yarn as much as a Common Heel does.

Heel shaping

***K10 (11:12:13:14:15:16:17), wrap next st, turn.

Row 1 P20 (22:24:26:28:30:32:34), wrap next st, turn. Slide other 22 (24:26:28:30:32:34:36) sts (sts between wrapped sts) onto spare needles.

Row 2 K19 (21:23:25:27:29:31:33), wrap next st, turn.

Row 3 P18 (20:22:24:26:28:30:32), wrap next st, turn. Cont in this way, wrapping one less st on each row before wrapping next st until the following row has been worked:
p6 (6:8:8:8:10:10:10), wrap next st, turn.

Next row K6 (6:8:8:8:10:10:10), work wrapped st, wrap next st, turn.

Next row P7 (7:9:9:9:11:11:11), work wrapped st, wrap next st, turn.

Next row K8 (8:9:9:9:12:12:12), work double-wrapped st by knitting through the st and the two wraps together, wrap next st, turn.

Next row P9 (9:11:11:11:13:13:13), work double-wrapped st by purling through the st and the two wraps together, wrap next st, turn.
Cont in this way, working one more st before wrapping next st on each row until the following row has been worked:
p19 (21:23:25:27:29:31:33), work double-wrapped st, wrap next st, turn.***

Next row/round K20 (22:24:26:28:30:32:34), work double-wrapped st, knit across 22 (24:26:28:30:32:34:36) sts held on spare needles, work remaining double-wrapped st, k10 (11:12:13:14:15:16:17).

Foot

You have a choice when knitting the foot of a sock: you can knit plain, smooth stockinette/stocking stitch or you can continue the pattern from the Cuff. If you choose to continue the pattern, decide whether it will be just on the top of the foot or run under the sole as well. Some patterns, like the spiral rib used in Do The Twist (see pages 114–117), will add cushioning, but others may rub delicate feet.

Whatever you choose, work the foot until the sock measures 4¾ (5½:6¼:6½:7:7½:7¾:8¼) in/12 (14:16: 17:18:19:20:21) cm from the back of the Heel.

▲ Wedge toe

▲ Short row toe

Toes

There are two types of knitted toe here, try them both and see which one suits your toes best.

Wedge toe

This style of toe has paired decreases on each side of the foot so that the sock tapers. The remaining stitches are then grafted together.

Start by placing markers 11 (12:13:14:15:16:17:18) sts either side at beginning and end of rounds – there will be two sets of 22 (24:26:28:30:32:34:36) sts divided by these markers.

Round 1 Knit to 3 sts before first marker, k2tog, k1 (marker), k1, ssk2tog, knit to 3 sts before next marker, k2tog, k1 (marker), k1, ssk2tog, knit to end.
Round 2 Knit.
Rep these two rounds until 20 (20:24:24:24:24:24) sts remain.
Knit to first marker.

Rearrange sts so that the first 5 (5:6:6:6:6:6:6) and last 5 (5:6:6:6:6:6:6) sts of the round are on one needle with the 10 (10:12:12:12:12:12:12) middle sts on another needle.
Graft toe together using Kitchener stitch (see page 10).

Short row toe

This is very similar to the Short row heel (see page 139) and is worked from the sole of the foot, over the toes and back to stitches left at the top of the foot. There are more stitches to graft than with the Wedge toe, but don't let that put you off: instructions are on page 10.

Work exactly as for Short row heel from *** to ***.

Next row/round K20 (22:24:26:28:30:32:34), work double-wrapped st.
Graft Toe stitches to those left on spare needles.

index

suppliers list

ThreadBear Fiber Arts Studio
319 S. Waverly Road
Lansing, MI 48917
Phone: 517-703-9276
Toll-Free: 866-939-2327
info@threadbearfiberarts.com
www.threadbearfiberarts.com

Yarn Lady
Oakbrook Village
Suite M 24371 Avenida De La Carlota
Laguna Hills, CA 92653
Phone: 949-770-7809
Toll-Free: 888-770-7809
yarn@yarnlady.com
www.yarnlady.com

String Yarns
130 East 82nd Street
New York, NY 10028
Phone: 212-288-9276
www.stringyarns.com

Needle Nook
705 N. Main Street
Moscow, ID 83843
Phone: 208-882-2033
questions@needlenookonline.com
www.needlenookonline.com

acknowledgements

I would like to thank the team of knitters –
Diane, Carie, Avril, Denis, Rachel, Shelley, Joy
and Christine – who knitted nothing but socks
for weeks and did a brilliant job. Thanks also goes
to everyone at Hamlyn, who do everything that
makes a book possible.

Executive Editor: Katy Denny
Editor: Camilla Davis
Pattern checker: Sue Whiting
Executive Art Editor: Penny Stock
Designer: Beverly Price, www.one2six.com
Photographer: Janine Hosegood
Production Manager: Manjit Sihra

picture credits

Special photography:
Octopus Publishing Group Ltd/Janine Hosegood